CGA

=

COMPETENCY

Competency is tied in to respect for teaching,

within the bounds of professional ethics.

My deep thanks to the translators

at Westminster Abbey Strategies, Inc.

AB + Publications

CGA

=

COMPETENCY

by

Sylvie Deslauriers, PhD, MSc

FCPA, FCA, CGA, FCMA, CPA (FL), CMA (US)

Professor of Accounting

University of Québec at Trois-Rivières

AB + Publications

CGA = COMPETENCY
by Sylvie Deslauriers, CGA, PhD

© 2013   AB + Publications

Graphics and Cover design: Sabina Kopica

AB⁺ Publications®

P.O. Box 38	10738 Sun Palm Lane
St-Alban	Suite #201
Quebec	Boynton Beach, Florida
CANADA	UNITED STATES
G0A 3B0	33437

info@ABplusPublications.com
www.ABplusPublications.com

ISBN 978-0-9918853-8-1 (paperback format)
ISBN 978-0-9738038-7-7 (*eBook-pdf* format)

Legal deposit: 2013
Library and Archives Canada
Bibliothèque et Archives nationales du Québec

OTHER BOOKS BY DR. SYLVIE DESLAURIERS:
   EA$Y $UCCE$$, AB + Publications.
      © 2013 ISBN 978-0-9738038-9-1 paperback (*eBook-pdf* 978-0-9918853-5-0) (*ePub 6-7*)
   Teaching Tips for Accounting Cases, AB + Publications.
      © 2012 ISBN 978-0-9738038-5-3 paperback (*eBook-pdf* 978-0-9918853-3-6)
   Accounting for Success The Guide to Case Resolution, AB + Publications.
      © 2010 ISBN 978-0-9738038-4-6 paperback (*eBook-pdf* 978-0-9918853-1-2)

PREFACE

Dear CGA candidates,

Based on my 28 years of experience in the teaching and professional marking of cases, it is with confidence that I present to you this volume. My objective quite simply is to guide you towards better success.

I personally chose to write the professional CGA examinations in 2009.

In a CGA's career path, the resolution of multidisciplinary cases is the culmination of several years of study in accounting. The resolution of cases requires, on the one hand, a great diversity of knowledge and, on the other hand, an ability to adapt to every-changing situations. Since each case is unique, each is a challenge in and of itself.

A case is a scenario which reflects events in practice. One must identify the stakes, and analyze them by referring to relevant knowledge which applies to this specific context, in order, ultimately, to take a position by making a finding or a recommendation, as part of a systematic problem-solving process and in a limited time frame.

In order to improve one's performance in case resolution, one must invest one's time in a disciplined manner. My volume CGA = COMPETENCY is intended to assist you in developing your ability to read, plan, draft, present, analyze, assess and study cases. The concepts involved are amply illustrated by relying on the Ajax Metals case set out in the appendix hereto, as well as in the numerous examples derived from an in-depth analysis of the CGA materials.

I am pleased to share with you the sum total of my work, in order to assist you in your own success.

Proud to be a CGA,

Dr. Sylvie Deslauriers

CONTENTS

Part 1
Reading a Case

The "Case Parameters"
Active Reading
Annotations

"A competency is a specific behavior whereby a professional applies knowledge, skills, and/or professional values in a work environment."

CGA Competency framework, CGA-Canada, 2010, p. 10

PART 1
Reading a Case[1]

Each case is unique. Each is made up of a set of characteristics which, together, distinguish it from all other cases. Indeed, a problem or issue to be resolved, a topic to be discussed or a calculation to be performed may be found in more than one case. However, the approach is different. Hence, since there can be no two identical cases, your ability to quickly adapt to any new situation guarantees your success.

The "Case Parameters"

Upon reading a case, one must, as soon as possible, flesh out those characteristics which make it unique, and which I refer to as the "case parameters": the "Required" elements, the "Role", and the "Context". Taken together, these parameters form a specific frame of reference which you must keep in mind throughout the resolution of the case. One must, therefore, identify, understand and use them. These case parameters are the following:

What is "Required"

This refers to what you are required to do. It is crucial to identify the list of problems or issues to be resolved, in order to draft a relevant response. At times, what is Required is clearly stated, if not directed, and at times, greater efforts must be spent defining it. In other words, what is the task with which you have been entrusted?

E.g.: Write a memo to the audit committee addressing the issues discovered during the audit.

The "Role"

In the great majority of cases, if not all of them, you are asked to play the role of a "newly certified" CGA[2]. Sometimes, you are the "accountant external to the organization" (PA1, AP1), and, at other times, you are "a financial manager internal to the organization" (PA2). In light of this starting point, you must identify more specifically what is the position held within the organization under study. What are your duties and responsibilities?

E.g.: As a public accountant, you can be specialized in small businesses or in not-for-profit organizations.

The "Context"

Under this heading, I include any specific information relating to the case under study. What is characteristic of the organization or its environment which does not necessarily appear in other cases? This information, which is often disparate, allows for a better understanding of what is occurring.

E.g.: The bank line of credit outstanding cannot exceed 75% of the value of inventories.

E.g.: This is a small business with only three employees outside the family.

---

1   In order to illustrate the concepts set out throughout this volume, illustrations taken from the Ajax Metals case (AJX CASE), outlined in Exhibit A, are used.

2   CGA syllabus, PA1, p. 87, PA2, p. 88

Active Reading

From the outset, allow me to state that reading a case is a very active process. One must not only read the facts or the financial data. One must understand them, relate them to each other, then classify them efficiently. Reading a case is a crucial step requiring that one devote one third to one fourth of the time allotted to the resolution thereof. Hence, for a 100-minute case, reading will account for 25 to 33 minutes.

Since the resolution of a case must take place within a restricted time frame – maybe even a tight deadline –, one must plan the reading stage in such a manner as to determine as quickly as possible that which is specific to the case. I suggest two steps: 1 Overview of the information provided and 2 Detailed reading of the text and the exhibits.

Overview of the Information Provided

The first thing to do is to read the Required section. There is no question that responding to the request of an employer or a client is essential to the success of a case. One must, therefore, carefully read this part – better twice than once – where each word is significant. Personally, I rewrite the words of the Required section on the left-hand page of the booklet in order to grasp as precisely as possible what is being requested.[1] Based on my experience, I know that it is easy to forget to respond to one or several of the questions asked – unfortunately, sometimes, one of the most important – and a proper reading of the Required section greatly reduces this risk. I have on occasion been able to confirm my understanding by going to read the definition of a word in the *Glossary of Assessment Terms* supplied with the examination questions. The term "Evaluate", for instance, means that I am being asked to "mak[e] an informed judgment based on knowledge and information".

> AJX CASE (A5)
>
> The Required section contains a list of questions which must all be identified and addressed. Rewriting the most significant words will enable you to highlight of them. Hence, "making recommendations on the **risks** associated with **relocating the manufacturing** of the products" means that one must identify these risks, within this specific decision of relocation, and make recommendations in order to mitigate or eliminate them.
>
> At some point in time, in one manner or another, one will be required to further specify the questions in the Required section, by identifying the topics or aspects to be discussed. However, it is definitely an asset to know, as of the first few minutes, that one must look for these risks while reading of the case.

On occasion, the wording of the Required section is not as specific as one would wish. For instance, the following sentence: "Write a letter to Jennifer addressing her concerns." is not very explicit. Once again, it is very useful to know from the outset that one is required to specify what these "concerns" are. This allows for a focusing of the reading of the case on what is essential.

In order to detect as soon as possible the problems or issues to be discussed, without necessarily conducting a detailed reading of the case, here are a few TIPS:

   ✆   Keep an eye out for the letters CGA within the text, the name of the recipient of the report or the designation you have been given. E.g.: "Jennifer's major concern is the inability of her organization to follow up on endowment contributions."

---

1   One could also use a worksheet or otherwise right directly on the case itself. Personally, I prefer to attach to my reply all the steps in my reasoning prior to commencing the drafting itself.

- Briefly look at the beginning of paragraphs. They may, for instance, start with a sentence such as: "Another issue is the renewal of the grant…".

- Identify the part of the text where the listing of the general information on the organization ceases and the presentation of the various problems or issues of the current period begins.

   AJX CASE: The heading "Current Issues" marks this division. (A3)

- Examine the structure of the text, since certain headings may, from the outset, point to a preliminary issue to be discussed. E.g.: "Internal Disagreements".

- Note the manner in which the information is presented. E.g.: by month, by product, by division (A9), etc. It is likely that the response will require you to take this structure into account.

COMMENT

Personally, when reading a case, I use tools in order to facilitate an eventual return to the text I have read. Since everything that deals with the Required elements is very important, I use a green highlighter in order to highlight those specific items, and I change colours for other information. Hence, no matter where the idea is expressed in the case, the colour green means that it is a component of the work to be performed. (A1 to A9)

If you have not already done so by this stage, you must ensure that you fully understand the role that you are asked to play. Of course, at the outset, you are a CGA professional. However, in order to determine the angle in which to approach the problems or issues, you must identify with greater specification the expertise required.

AJX CASE (A5)

In the case, the role to be played is not the same in a. and in b. Indeed, you are required to act as an accountant external to the organization, however the requests in a. and b. require a different expertise. Under a., the accountant is a consultant and, under b., he is an external auditor.

Consequently, let us assume, for instance, that there is a "negative cash balance" (A6). The external consultant will consider the impact of this risk on the plans for the relocation of manufacturing via the acquisition of new equipment (A23). As for the external auditor, he will consider this fact when making his decision to accept the engagement (A28) and in his assessment of the going concern problem. (A30)

Thereafter, one must briefly scan the contents of the exhibits, if any, with a view to identifying the material placed at your disposal in order to resolve the case. For instance, the presence of an exhibit providing three "divisional income statements" means that there will probably be differences to outline between the divisions (A9). Similarly, a heading such as "New Privacy Policy" will probably mean that you will be required to comment the contents of this new policy.

Detailed Reading of the Text

The first few paragraphs of a case usually provide general information on the organization under study: its history, its market, its mission, its shareholders, its organizational structure, etc. As mentioned above, among the case parameters of a case is what is specific to its "context". One must, therefore, if need be, identify the following items: the size of the organization, the industry sector, the key success factors, the strengths, the weaknesses, opportunities and threats, the objectives, needs, preferences, bias and responsibilities of stakeholders, constraints, the business policies, the features of managerial behaviour, etc. Any one of these items of information could be useful to explain a problem, analyze an issue or otherwise substantiate a recommendation. For instance, knowing that the organization wishes to minimize the costs of the inputs will be a factor in the decision-making process which is relevant to the selection of a supplier.

AJX CASE (A1)

In the case, it is crucial to identify the following, among others:

- "AJX is an international supplier", since that implies the existence of foreign currency transactions as well as the presence of different laws and tax rules.
- "AJX manufactures three types of chemicals", since usually it is an industry sector which is riskier than most.
- "AJX's management and board of directors monitor the decisions and activities of all of its subsidiaries", since such a centralization policy describes the nature of relations between the entities.

COMMENT

Personally, I write down clearly in my booklet the list of items in the context in order to be able to rapidly refer to them. Indeed, they may be useful more than once in drafting the response.

It sometimes happens as well that they are not useful at all. Note, for instance, that the "… divisions have been operating near capacity for several years" is a relevant factor to identify. However, when you read a little further along, the threat to the effect that "… in Ontario, sales are expected to decrease significantly" makes the former information obsolete. (A3)

In addition to the foregoing, a detailed reading, on the one hand, allows one to further specify the problems or issues to be addressed in the Required section and, on the other hand, to highlight the information that you may require in order to resolve them. Hence, throughout the reading, one must continue to specify that which must be done while paying attention to any indication of a request on the part of the employer or the client. Any suggestion or method contemplated by the recipient of the report must be identified and analysed, even if you know in advance this is not a good idea. Your client may believe, for instance, that the amount of dividends received is the best measure of the profitability of his or her business. You will be required to disabuse him/her of this notion, explain why, and then suggest other action.

Indeed, one must identify all that is different or has just occurred, in particular during the current period. When reading the case, you must constantly ask yourself: What are the problems or the issues to be solved? What issues have not been resolved? What is wrong with the organization? What is in flux? For that reason, for instance, a heading such as "Current Issues" must draw your attention (A3). Also, the topic of "Leasing or purchasing the equipment" is to be added to the items to be approached under the Required section "tax issues that might be involved in creating separate subsidiaries" (A5).

> **One must identify all issues that are outstanding, since they will all usually require resolution.**

The problems or issues to be resolved are often clearly identified by an appropriate sentence, such as "An important issue is…" or "There is a pressing issue…". One must pay particular attention to requests originating from the intended audience. A sentence such as: "The Vice-President is considering closing a manufacturing plant…" must attract your attention. Throughout the reading of the case, one must also realize that each paragraph sets out a different problem or issue.

One must also be aware of the fact that the problems or issues, or even topics to be discussed, will not always be set out in obvious fashion. One could refer to them as non-directed questions. In the AJX case, in Exhibit 4-5, one must identify the fact that the profitability of the various products may not be the same. (A9)

Finally, one must be conscious of the possibility that a single fact in the case may have multiple implications. The implementation of a new computer system, for instance, may have impacts on the job description of the employees, the type of reports generated and inventory management. Similarly, note that in Exhibit 4-5 "backups for data starting July 1 have not yet been located" (A9) gives rise to three different issues: "need for timely, reliable information" (A17), "need for a reliable backup system" (A21) and "need to avoid a scope limitation" (A29).

Detailed Reading of the Exhibits

By the time you read the exhibits, you already have a good idea of the important problems or issues to be discussed. We already know what is Required, what role you are asked to play, and what the particulars of the context of the organization under study are. A detailed reading of the exhibits is, therefore, a process that occurs once the case parameters are essentially known and understood. Consequently, this reading is more directed to that which will be relevant to the resolution of the case. For instance, knowing that "AJX needs to invest in new equipment for $3 million" (A4), you will pay greater attention to its financial position.

Once the financial statements of an organization are presented, one must learn to flesh out the key aspects within a restricted time frame. The information provided, among others, is used to determine or better understand the topics to be approached, to justify certain ideas or otherwise to highlight a new problem or issue. By examining the financial information supplied in the exhibit, one must constantly take into account that which is Required. One must also flesh out any relation with any of the case facts previously identified.

Examples of items drawn from
the Financial information exhibits to highlight

Items to highlight	Examples (AJX CASE)
Basic information	– 2010 unaudited – Year ended November 30 (Mexico segment June 30!)
Most significant items (in terms of percentage, variations, and risk)	Net cash provided by operating activities is positive while the items Cash and cash equivalents and Short-term investments have decreased since 2009. Investing activities was financed through short-term funds!
Patterns, relationships, and trends	The Foreign exchange losses of the current year ($1,200) are almost as important than Net earnings of $1,574. In fact, the decrease in the 2010 profitability is clearly explained by those losses. N.B.: Take a quick look at the usual relations such as revenues/receivables, cost of goods sold/inventories, commissions/sales, etc.
Unusual items	The long-term loan of $9,436 (+ current portion of $1,534) is entirely payable to a related party.
Inconsistencies and contradictions	For 2009 and 2010, the overall gross margin is stable at 38%. However, it varies from 6% to 40% at the divisional level!
Non-compliance with accounting standards, laws or business policies	Pricing policy is supposed to provide a steady profit level (A3). However, Mexico profitability is really low compared to the others.
Key ratios	– The working capital ratio has significantly decreased since 2009. – The gross margin ratio can be calculated to make a comparison between the divisions.

COMMENT

When faced with financial statements, several candidates do not truly know how to structure their reading. I then remind them of the following categories: liquidity, leverage, profitability and activity. Indeed, that does not cover all that is set out in the table above, but this starting point allows for a diversification of your observations.

On the one hand, certain candidates read all the items of the financial statements in detail or automatically calculate a series of ratios. They waste precious time in doing so. As explained above, one must quickly focus on the essential.

Where an exhibit sets out other financial information than the financial statements, one must flesh out that which is important, and remember to analyze the data from three points of view: patterns, relationships and trends. For instance, where the schedule sets out a "Summary of unadjusted misstatements", one must be aware of the fact that it is impossible to analyze each of the items found therein. One must, therefore, during the reading stage, identify those items that are the most significant, or the most specifically related to a problem or issue to be resolved.

Where an exhibit deals with a single topic, its title is therefore precise and refers directly to a problem or issue to be dealt with. For instance, knowing that the exhibit deals with the salient point identified following a visit by a Revenue Canada Agency auditor will facilitate the drafting of your response since all the necessary information will be found in the same section.

It sometimes occurs as well that one happens upon an exhibit that I would characterize as being "miscellaneous" since it contains information on various topics. For instance, it could contain extracts from a conversation or excerpts from a meeting. Under such circumstances, you should carefully read each of the paragraphs contained therein, since they will complement your understanding of what is going on. As you read, I suggest that you identify in writing the problems or issues tackled in each paragraph. In my view, this is essential in order to minimize the time you waste during the drafting of the response. I will revisit this issue in the following section on annotations.

Finally, I emphasize the fact that one must read the case in its entirety before going on to the planning stage and the drafting of the response. You must perform a focused and active reading up to the last word of the last exhibit, in particular because you must understand the connections between the various items of information. For instance, note that the AJX case contains two non-directed questions on the last page! (A9)

Annotations

We have just seen how to read a case and what information to focus on during the reading. I would now like to explain to you how to make annotations. Even though I devote a separate section to them, annotations form an integral part of the detailed reading of a case. Annotating a case is to classify information and to identify those case facts which will be useful to the drafting of the response. Since you do not have time to summarize or to copy the case, you must make sure to be able to retrieve any useful case facts quickly and efficiently.

Pages A2 to A9 illustrate the manner in which I annotate a case. This is a summary of what I suggest:

- *Identify the case parameters.* Anything that relates to the Required items is highlighted in green, the role is identified and the list of items specific to the context is set out in the booklet. (see top of A10)

- *Save the left-hand margin of the case in order to flag any Required items.* Write out the problem or issue or the topic to be dealt with, and add a reference to a. or b. Since this margin will only contain that which is requested, this will simplify the planning of your answer and ensure that you have not forgotten anything. Of course, one must flag those areas which will be used in respect of more than one question.

| **Primary (important) – Secondary** | Adding signs such as "IMP" or "+++", *versus* "+/-", allows you to identify from the outset those problems or issues that are the most prominent. Since the resolution of the case must be performed within a restricted time frame, one had better know what are the better topics that must absolutely be dealt with and those that one might have to set aside. |

◷ *Write brief comments in the right-hand margin* in order to enable a quick location of the particulars of the case. For instance, one could write key words such as "regulations" (A3) or "interco" (A4), or a brief opinion such as "steady profit level? not really!". (A9)

◷ *Identify those sections which may be useful in the resolution of the problems or issues,* where the circumstances allow you to do so. For instance, the abbreviation "R" is used to identify "risks associated with relocating the manufacturing of the products". (A4)

Advantages (ADV) – **Disadvantages (DIS)** **Risks (R) –** **Opportunities (O)**	Writing "ADV" (or "+") and "DIS" (or "–") next to the arguments set out in the case will allow for a quicker analysis of the benefits and disadvantages of a make-or-buy decision, for instance.

◷ *Identify the relations between the various items of information.* For instance, there are several words or expressions, such as "may attract", "may become possible", "indirectly sell" and "informal survey", which demonstrate uncertainty relating to the sale of the Liquified product to the agricultural producers. Hence, "lot of uncertainties!" is a strong integrative comment which it is useful to write in the margin. (A4)

Specifically, one must flesh out the links between the financial information contained in the exhibits and in the text of the case. Suppose, for instance, that you are provided with a list of "industry selected ratios" in a schedule. Since you know, after having read page 2 of the case, that the organization's target is an annual growth in sales of 20%, you can already underline this ratio in order to use it as a benchmark in the analysis.

Finally, one must pay attention to anything repeated, similar and synchronous, as well as to any inconsistencies and contradictions. For instance, an observation on several occasions that there are intercompany transactions is, in and of itself, an indication that this topic will be required to be broached in your response. (A3, A4, A8)

> **Reading a case is not strictly a linear process since, on occasion, one must backtrack in order to perfect one's understanding of what is going on.**

◷ *Draw little diagrams where the information appears to you not to be clear,* such as the position of John in the history of AJX (A5) or the manufacturing production of one country as opposed to another (A4). This allows you to observe that two of the three company relocations will be directed towards Mexico.

Under certain circumstances, drawing a diagram of the parties involved, drawing a temporal line retracing the key events or the journal entries of a complex transaction may facilitate your understanding of the situation. Personally, retracing the movement of accounting documents from one department to the next, for instance, appears to me to be clearer when one draws a diagram.

COMMENT

There are many methods of annotating a case and, in this volume, I am sharing with you the fruit of my personal experience. Try several methods out and establish your method of work in light of your personality. What is important is that your annotations will facilitate the flagging of relevant case facts during the drafting of your response. You will not have the opportunity to reread the case twice. It is therefore crucial, during the reading thereof, to give yourself the means of annotating the text and the exhibits in a clear and efficient manner.

- *Read a paragraph in its entirety* – or at least a significant part thereof –, *take a step back and highlight what is truly useful*. Otherwise, the entire text might appear in yellow highlighter! You must select the words or expressions that you would like to stress. For instance, the word "**recently**" means that reference is being made to an event that occurred during the current fiscal year and must be considered. Also, certain words such as "**new** system in place", "**key** donors", "**no formal** control on…", "the system has been developed by the **clerk**", etc., must draw your attention. You must also focus on words that characterize a situation, such as "**failure** to meet budget", "recent economic slowdown has **severely** affected", "the company has **unsuccessfully** tried to …", etc.

  Finally, one must observe that there are "**three** sources of financing", "**two** covenant clauses", "**three** types of inventory", "**two** stores, but **one** is really more important than the other", etc.

- *Limit the number of annotations on the case / on the examination paper itself.* They are only for your personal use and will, under no circumstances, be considered in the assessment of your response. Abbreviate your annotations, since you are the only person using them.

  One should be reasonable in the selection of the annotations in order not to overburden the text and get lost. One must also adjust to the circumstances of the case. For instance, it could happen that the regular reference to the "$" symbol or the word "flow" in the margin will enable you to flag with efficiency everything that must be considered as part of a computation to be performed.

- Do not start drafting your answer prior to having completed the reading of the case. If you are afraid of forgetting an observation, an idea, a comment or a short calculation, it is always possible to write it very briefly on the left-hand page of your booklet.

One must read a case with objectivity, and without ascribing to words a meaning which they do not have. In other words, you must confine your analysis to that which is written, black on white, without adding any words. Also, you must consider that which is unwritten, not done or does not exist. For instance, you could read the sentence "These sales may become possible by allowing agricultural producers to indirectly sell these products". (A4) But you should not conclude that direct selling is automatically possible, since there is no indication to that effect in the case. As well, one should not surmise that markets other than that of agricultural producers exist. Without any indication to that effect, it would be pure speculation.

© CGA = COMPETENCY

Part 2
Planning One's Response

The List of Problems or Issues to be Resolved
The Significance of Problems or Issues
The Cover Page

"Prioritizing multiple problems is vital, as is recognizing their scope."

CGA Competency framework, CGA-Canada, 2010, p. 13

12

PART 2
Planning One's Response

Prior to beginning the drafting of a response to a case, I suggest that you plan the time you have left. Establishing a response plan, whether in writing or in your head, will help you to better succeed. This does not mean that you already know all that you will write, but rather that the problems or issues have been determined, then prioritized, in light of the role you have been asked to play and of the Required elements.

The List of Problems or Issues to be Resolved

It appears to me to be essential to see the big picture with respect to the problems or issues to be resolved in order to correctly plan the breadth and depth of analysis of the various topics. Personally, to this end, I take short notes all throughout the reading of the case. An example of such notes, for the AJX case, appears on page A10. When one examines these written notes on the left-hand page of the booklet, one can observe the following:

- Writing each question asked as a caption is a reminder of that which is required. In this manner, one makes sure not to forget anything. There are, therefore, for instance, under a. five questions which must be answered. If, for instance, nothing were to be written under the heading "ASSISTANCE TO METALLO MX", then one would have to seek to identify the topic or topics to be dealt with.

- The requests are divided into segments a. and b. in order to facilitate drafting. This separation between the two parts is to be taken into account since the role to be played, the intended recipient or even the person preparing the report – as in the AJX case –, may be different.

- Throughout the reading, the topics to be discussed have been written down. Therefore, they appear on the worksheet in the order in which they were identified. Naturally, the significance of a topic as opposed to another may be specified therein, such as the GOING CONCERN problem.

> **COMMENT**
>
> Personally, when I identify the problems or issues to be resolved, I highlight certain topics. For this reason, for instance, the ethical issues are listed separately.
>
> I would do the same for a situation of potential fraud, professional negligence on the part of a colleague or the existence of unusually high business risks.

- One observes that certain topics are repeated in more than one column. This means that a topic, such as the presence of intercompany transactions, must be examined from several angles: the consolidation of subsidiaries with the parent (Financial accounting, A16), the tax implications (Taxation, A17), as well as additional related parties' disclosures under International Financial Reporting Standards (IFRS) (Financial Accounting, A27).

COMMENT

One must understand that the context in which the discussion is to be taking place must be considered. The angle from which to approach the discussion of the presence of intercompany transactions, for instance, changes if one examines it from the accounting point of view or from the taxation point of view. While it is true that both aspects may be discussed one after the other, it will be separately. Mixing the discussion of the accounting and the taxation of intercompany transactions in the same paragraph would not be a good way of proceeding. The drafting would run the risk of not sufficiently distinguishing between the two aspects.

I, therefore, suggest rewriting the topic under each question requested in order to remind oneself of each of the aspects to be discussed.

- If need be, the interrelations between the topics are underlined. As mentioned above, one must reply to each question asked and usually independently. One must, thereafter, take a step back and search for the existence of connections between the topics. The presence of a negative cash flow (A6), for instance, increases the risks associated with relocating the manufacturing. This also casts some doubt on the going concern; this doubt will have to be assessed by the auditor.

- It occurs quite frequently that case facts may be used to identify or resolve more than one problem or issue. The fact, for instance, that the "Mexican economy could experience significant inflation in the next few years" (A4) must be considered as part of the discussion of the accounting issues AND in terms of risks associated with relocating the manufacturing.

COMMENT

The scope of the reading notes varies from one case to the next, in light, among others, of the difficulty of retracing the information. The 100 minute comprehensive AJX case includes several questions to be resolved, that have been allocated between a. and b. Organizing the information in columns allows one to see the big picture of what needs to be done.

When you are faced with a short 50 minute case, the notes are usually much more succinct, and may remain in part in your head. Also, where the case is one that is more directed or has no exhibits, written annotations on the case itself sometimes suffice.

As you will recall, it is essential to organize the information contained in the case in order to properly understand what is going on and to adequately establish the list of problems or issues to be resolved. The manner of annotating a case or filling out a worksheet may be different in one case as opposed to another, and from one person to the next, but the objective, insofar as its usefulness is concerned, remains the same.

Before commencing the drafting of your response, I suggest that you take a step back and ask yourself if there may be any problems or issues which you may have missed. As you will have guessed, this usually involves "non-directed questions". In other words, at this stage, you must ensure that you actually possess the list of all that which must be resolved. By way of illustration, the fact that "foreign currency translation" is a topic involved in creating separate subsidiaries does not, perhaps, stand out clearly at first glance (A10). Therefore, one must mark a pause and ask oneself whether, in light of the case facts, there are any topics that need to be added.

14

I wish to draw your attention to the fact that a problem or issue to be discussed must always originate from the case under study. One cannot, therefore, discuss anything one wishes based on the premise that it might, directly or indirectly, affect an organization. One must, therefore, remember to constantly take into account the case parameters. In this respect, one must also ensure that the response plan does not contain useless topics.

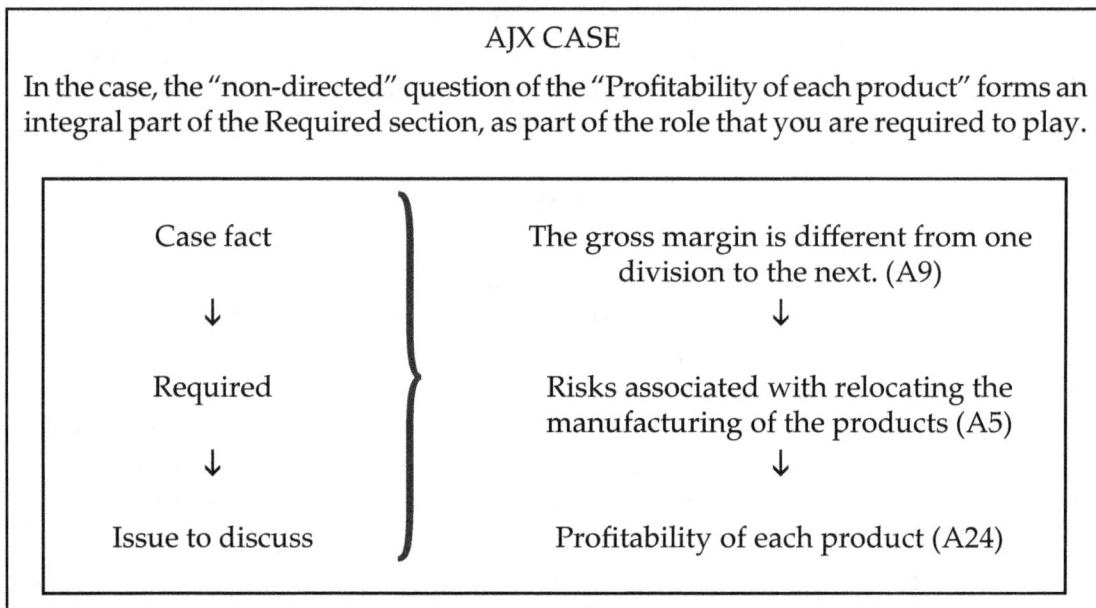

AJX CASE

In the case, the "non-directed" question of the "Profitability of each product" forms an integral part of the Required section, as part of the role that you are required to play.

Case fact	The gross margin is different from one division to the next. (A9)
↓	↓
Required	Risks associated with relocating the manufacturing of the products (A5)
↓	↓
Issue to discuss	Profitability of each product (A24)

Under certain circumstances, one must know how to detect and add up the case facts pointing in the same direction in order to be able to identify a problem or issue which is more important or more prominent than the others. The difficulty resides in the detection of these case facts which do not always appear obvious upon a reading of the case. One must, therefore, at some point in time, take a step back in order to see the "big picture". It is possible, for instance, that an initial case fact did not draw your attention but that it becomes wholly significant when placed in relation to one or several other case facts that follow. Hence, one may come to suspect a "potential fraud", to identify a "going concern problem", to observe that "financial information has been manipulated", to establish that there is "insufficient corporate governance" or to question the "independence of the previous auditor".

AJX CASE	
Metallo's management is considering producing the Standard product in Mexico where no bans on pesticides for cosmetic purposes exist. (A4)	Metallo management feels that the Industrial product would be better manufactured in Mexico due to more business-friendly regulations. (A4)

Ethical issue (A20)

N.B.: The fact that AJX is considering relocating its products to Mexico on two occasions rather than one is, in and of itself, a case fact that must be picked up on.

COMMENT

Certain candidates make a list of potential problems or issues, of an integrative or other nature, that can be found in the cases. For instance, between the reading of the case and the drafting of the response, they will systematically ask themselves if the requirements of the stakeholders must be considered in the response.

I have nothing against this tactic which is intended to ensure that a significant aspect has not escaped my attention. However, one must be prudent. One should not deal with the requirements of the stakeholders in each case and, as you no doubt know, that depends on the circumstances of each case.

Should you ask yourself the question? Definitely.

Should you launch into the discussion without a valid case fact? NO.

I remind you, incidentally, that the various competencies developed during the program do not automatically find their way into each case. It would, therefore, be inappropriate to "force", for instance, a tax discussion in any event.

The Significance of Problems or Issues

When one examines initially – and the same goes as well for a subsequent examination – the list of problems or issues to be resolved on page A10, one must agree that many things need to be done in a restricted time frame. On the one hand, one must know that certain problems or issues are more important than others and it appears to me significant to identify them in order to maximize one's success. On the other hand, one must also be cognizant of the fact that one must not necessarily discuss all the items listed under the heading "risks of relocating", for instance, in order to provide an adequate discussion regarding this issue.

As soon as it is possible to do so, I suggest you prioritize the various problems or issues in order to be already in a position to form an idea of the structure of your response. One could state that the problems or issues must be classified as follows: the primary issues and the secondary issues. In the resolution of a case, it appears to me to be essential to deal with – or at least to attempt to deal with – all the primary problems or issues (important) and some of the others. The prioritization of topics requires the exercise of a professional judgment. One must examine the information received and ask oneself what is important for the employer or the client, in light of the case parameters.

ASPECTS TO TAKE INTO ACCOUNT WHEN PRIORITIZING

Aspects to take into account	Examples
Amount of money involved Tip: For an item to be ranked as important, it must be valued at between 5% and 15% (or more) of the reference item—net income, revenues, total assets. Note: Impact on stakeholders is sometimes taken into account.	– The question asks for an analysis of the variations between the actual amounts and the budgeted amounts of some ten expenditure items. Due to a lack of time, it is not necessary to analyze all the items one after the other. One must rather detect which are the most significant variations, possibly three, may be four. – The organization currently has a debt covenant requiring a working capital ratio of no less than 1.5:1. The actual ratio is 1.6:1. All the accounts receivable likely to give rise to an allowance for doubtful accounts which would lead to a breach of the clause, become important, regardless of the size of the net income.
Risks involved Tip: You should note the possibility of risks involved with the item you are discussing. Will this item create major cash inflows or outflows? Could that change your conclusion or recommendation? Will it require estimates?	– As part of his audit, the auditor will consider that the determination of the value of the patent item in the amount of $500,000 is more difficult to establish than the valuation of the land item in the same amount. Indeed, the uncertainty associated with the nature of the asset itself increases the risks of misstatement. – The comptroller has just observed that some of the employees of the warehouse may have stolen merchandise. While he cannot, for the time being, assess the amount in question, it is a significant issue. On the other hand, the actual amount of this theft may ultimately be high and, on the other hand, the situation discloses the existence of internal control weaknesses which must absolutely be corrected.
Time factor Tip: Check out deadline or due date of subject. The nearer the date, the more likely it is to have greater importance.	– The backups for data have not yet been located (A9). In the short term, one must recover the financial data for the last five months for the division in Mexico. In the long term, a regular backup and recovery of data process will have to be developed. However, it is less urgent to solve this aspect which, therefore, requires a less in-depth discussion (A21). – If a decision to purchase or lease equipment has not yet been made, it becomes relevant to conduct an analysis of the benefits and disadvantages, and to conclude by making a substantiated recommendation, since it is still possible to influence the decision-making process. On the other hand, if the lease contract was executed last month, the matter has already been settled. Since this decision has already been made, there is no point in questioning it. It is too late to change anything.

Aspects to take into account	Examples
The specifics of the industry Tip: You should determine the main characteristics of the organization's business segment. What is special about this segment that you will not necessarily find elsewhere?	– One must note the fact that an organization is considering relocating the manufacturing in countries with more business-friendly regulations (A4). This fact takes on even greater significance in the AJX case, since chemical products are involved and public health is at issue. – The mission statement is very important for a non-profit organization; it determines the organization's strategic direction. One must take it into account when assessing the efficiency of the various programs offered or establishing non-financial performance measures.
The space given to a specific item Warning: Be careful about this one and look substance over form.	– There is an Exhibit presenting a list of the key performance indicators of the industry. It would probably be necessary to use the data contained therein as a benchmark in the performance of the organization under study. – During the reading of the case, several case facts with respect to the work of the sales manager can be observed. Repeated case facts are, in and of itself, a signal to, for instance, ask oneself questions as to the merits of the decisions which he has made over the last few months. N.B.: Generally, in order to enable a more in-depth analysis, one can state that a case will contain a greater number of case facts on a significant topic.

AJX CASE

In the case, several risk factors can be identified under the heading "risks associated with relocating the manufacturing"(A10). When comes the time to resolve this issue, I am, in actual fact, able to list up to six or seven different risk factors. The presence of these many factors which may be analyzed is, in and of itself, an indication of the significance of the issue. While considering that fact, one must, nevertheless, be conscious of the limited time frame allotted for a case and the need to tackle the other primary problems or issues. One must, therefore, restrict oneself to identifying and explaining the most significant risks, say at least three. You must trust in yourself and make a selection, and then draft efficiently. Time permitting, and if you deem your answer to be otherwise incomplete, you may briefly refer to these other risk factors that you have deemed to be of lesser importance.

Personally, in the AJX case, I consider that the three most significant risk factors are the following: lack of a cost/benefit analysis, cash flow problems and inflation. I would, therefore, draft my response in light of this selection.
N.B.: The ethical considerations related to public health are analyzed separately.

I reiterate that one must focus on what is essential when comes the time to resolve a case. In an ideal world, we would like to present a complete response taking into account all the risk factors detected, for instance. However, since time is limited, one must concentrate on that which is THE MOST IMPORTANT. Allow me to remind you that, in order to succeed in a case, one must show a good understanding of the key issues in the case.

At this stage, I would like to draw to your attention the following relations:

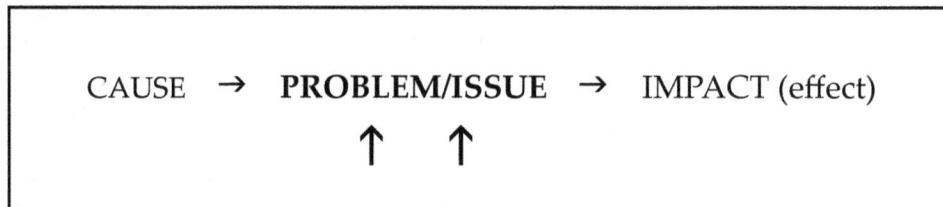

CAUSE → **PROBLEM/ISSUE** → IMPACT (effect)
↑   ↑

At the stage of planning the resolution of a case, one seeks to determine which problems or issues must be resolved. One must regularly exercise judgment in order to correctly interpret, from the outset, the significance of the case facts. Too often, candidates confuse cause, problem and impact. Otherwise, they do not correctly identify the actual cause of what is going wrong. The tip I give is to ask oneself if the actions you are contemplating taking will truly solve the outstanding problem. For instance, assume that the reports generated by the new information system contain errors. Prior to reaching the conclusion that the employees do not understand the system or determining that there are bugs in the new system, one must take the time to identify what the true cause of the problem is. What must one do in order to avoid any further problems in the reports? Taking a few seconds to reflect may enable you to draft a much more useful response.

Ensure that you use the time allotted efficiently.

Where the significance of the problems or issues has been established, I suggest that you focus briefly on planning the drafting of your response. In my opinion, one must have some idea of the time that you may devote to each of the problems or issues, so as to ensure an appropriate coverage of all the Required elements. If you have not given this aspect any thought, you run the real risk of analyzing the two or three first topics presented in too great a degree of depth at the expense of the latter topics.

When you are ready to commence a drafting of the response, between two thirds and three quarters of the total time allotted ought to be remaining, that is to say 67 to 75 minutes for a 100 minute case. Without falling into the trap of an excessive minute-by-minute planning, one must, nevertheless, have some idea of the time available for the resolution of each of the problems or issues. In other words, one must have in mind certain markers to indicate when time has come to conclude an analysis before going on to the next.

> **AJX CASE**
>
> In this case, the number of words allotted may be a useful guide in order to estimate that we have approximately 45 minutes left (70 minutes x 900/1,500 words) for Part a. and 25 minutes for Part b. We could also, generally speaking, allow for some 10 minutes for the treatment of each of the seven problems or issues identified. This is already a good starting indication.
>
> Thereafter, we could determine, for instance, that the issues of "reporting period for subsidiaries" and "assistance to Metallo MX" will be resolved in quicker fashion than the others. Therefore, we have an opportunity to analyze in greater depth a problem or issue among those appearing in Part a., such as "risks associated with relocating".

COMMENT

You have probably already guessed that planning a response to a 50 minute case is easier. The topics to be discussed are not as many, they are characterized by fewer interrelations and are often more directly set out in the case. You can, therefore, move on to the resolution of problems or issues at a quicker pace.

Regardless of the length of the case in question, remember that it is essential to provide an adequate coverage of the problems or issues while devoting greater depth of coverage to that which is important.

Finally, remember the two following cautionary notes:

- IMPORTANCE and DEPTH do not always go hand in hand. One must approach the important topics, early rather than later on in one's response, but it sometimes happens that one of the two may be quickly resolved. It would, therefore, be useless to drag the discussion on without any valid grounds.

    AJX CASE: The elimination of intercompany transactions during the consolidation process is an important financial accounting topic in creating separate subsidiaries. However, the resolution of this topic only requires three lines! (A11)

- TOPICS and SUB-TOPICS must be distinguished. The fact that a topic is important does not automatically mean that each aspect of said topic is also similarly important.

    E.g.: The Required elements ask for a discussion of the method of accounting for the new transactions in the fiscal year. The acquisition of a new warehouse, at a cost of $700,000, is a significant topic to be discussed. However, that does not necessarily imply that one must also discuss the manner of accounting for the anticipated betterment works in the amount of $30,000. It is possible that other more significant topics will take precedence.

**One must balance DEPTH and BREADTH
in order to analyse a case successfully.**

The Cover Page

Usually, where the Required elements require you to draft a memo (or a report), the cover page of your response ought to begin with the following sections:

```
                        MEMORANDUM

  Date:

  To:

  From: ..., CGA

  Subject: (or Re:)
```

In addition to the fact that these sections increase the professional appearance of your response, this manner of broaching the topic forces you to properly situate the case parameters. Hence, one must determine the **Date** of the preparation of your report. The **TO** section identifies who the report is aimed at (board of directors, client, senior partner, etc.) and the role (**From**) to be played during the simulation (audit manager, external consultant, comptroller, chief internal auditor, etc.). Properly identifying the contents of these sections from the outset represents a true asset in the drafting of your response. For instance, your request asking you to "explain the audit planning" will not be handled in the same manner if the date on which you conducted this planning is before or after the period end. The last area relates to the Topics of the report in itself (**Subject**), as summarized in one or two sentences. Personally, I attempt, to the extent possible, to copy the key words of the Required section in a succinct manner. Following the section, one should set out a brief introductory sentence – rarely more than two lines – starting, for instance, with the words "Please find attached…" or by the words "I have provided…".

Where the Required elements request that you "write a letter", the contents of the sections outlined above – Date, To, From, Re – must be revisited. Hence, one uses a letterhead, which is clear, short and directed in order to present the information in the appropriate format. One must also add one's signature after a brief conclusion at the bottom of the letter. As illustrated in the AJX CASE, each of the Parts a. and b. of the Required elements must be approached separately (A11, A14).

COMMENT

Personally, I prepare the cover page of my response as I am reading the case. This avoids me having to rewrite information or to search for such information once I start drafting.

There is no doubt that it is necessary to show one's "Communications" skills by appropriately presenting one's response. One must, however, be clear and succinct, merely owing to the fact that the time allotted as part of a case is restricted. There is no need to present a sophisticated introduction. One should minimize, if not do away with, usual trivialities, forms of polite address which contain no idea in response to the request set out in the case.

It is essentially the contents – and not the container – of your response which will determine your success.

Part 3
Drafting Relevant Ideas

Required ideas

Integrated ideas

Useful recommendations and conclusions

"Case questions give you an opportunity to integrate and apply your professional judgment to realistic and typical situations faced by a newly certified CGA."

Introduction to Strategic Financial Measurement, Course description and purpose, PA2, CGA-Canada, 2012-2013.

PART 3
Drafting Relevant Ideas

The response to a case purports, first and foremost, to be a response to the requests of an employer or a client. Each case is a scenario where a CGA professional acts with competence and diligence in the resolution of the problems or issues of an organization. It is clear that your response must contain relevant ideas, namely ideas that fit within the case parameters. In other words, one must constantly ensure that one is responding to the Required elements, in light of the role you have been asked to play and of the particulars of the case.

Required ideas

When solving a problem or issue, in order to ensure that you have submitted a complete response, I suggest you consider the following drafting structure:

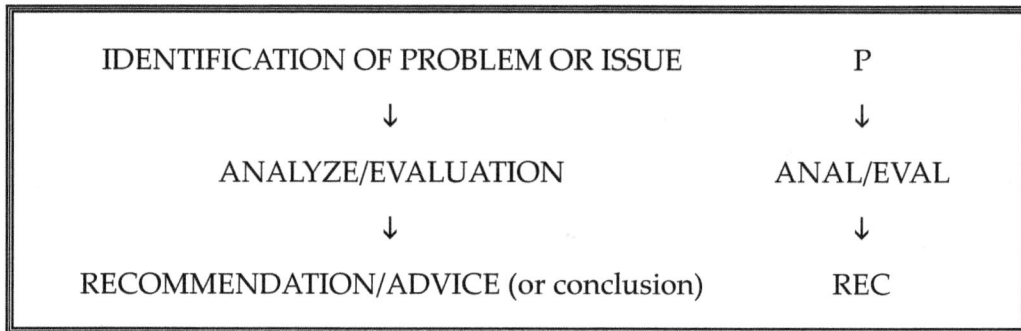

IDENTIFICATION OF PROBLEM OR ISSUE	P
↓	↓
ANALYZE/EVALUATION	ANAL/EVAL
↓	↓
RECOMMENDATION/ADVICE (or conclusion)	REC

From the very outset, it appears to me to be crucial to identify clearly what the PROBLEM or ISSUE to be resolved is. I insist on this point since it is the starting point of any analysis. Where the problem or issue is poorly defined, the discussion that follows will be much less relevant since it will be lacking the desired direction. For instance, thinking that the problem bears on the "compensation plan" does not generate the same discussion as thinking the problem is about "motivation among employees". Personally, I attempt to frame the problem or issue as clearly as possible in the title of each part that I am drafting.

COMMENT

It is not infrequent that a problem or issue is clearly mentioned in the case. In such an event, it also often appears as a title.

However, it does happen that we are required to diagnose the existence of a problem or issue, of a non direct or implicit nature, such as suspecting the existence of fraud, for instance. In such circumstances, one must do more than merely identify the existence of the problem. Explaining the causes thereof or justifying its importance may be an integral part of the analysis.

The ANALYZE/EVALUATION section takes on various forms, in light of the problem or issue to be resolved. You may, for instance, be called upon to discuss the impacts of a problem you have identified, to describe what the tax treatment of certain transactions will be, to assess the effects of the changes on the business processes, to compare the financial situation of the organization to the industry, to analyze the current budgetary process, to plan the next audit, etc. In point of fact, you are asked to expatiate on the topic in question in order to assist the employer or client in understanding or improving its/his/her current position.

> **The depth of analysis depends on the importance of the topic.**

Usually, one concludes a discussion of a problem or issue by providing one or several items of RECOMMENDATION/ADVICE. Indeed, any analysis must lead to a conclusion. A discussion of an independence problem as part of the acceptance of the audit engagement must, for instance, lead to a recommendation of a safeguard. Alternatively, a discussion of the tax implications of personal benefits to shareholders must bring about a conclusion as to the tax treatment. As for me, knowing in advance what the conclusion of the discussion will be helps me concentrate on what is essential.

The next page will set out a series of examples illustrating the contents of this drafting structure.

When comes time to commence drafting, several candidates experience difficulty in generating ideas or in determining if their discussion is complete. To this end, I suggest that you think of the following questions:

To remember to:	Questions	Examples
Justify one's ideas or recommendations	**WHY?** due to... given... because... in order to...	– AJX must adopt IFRS for January 2011 because it is publicly traded. (A14) – The audit risk is higher due to the difficult situation of two major clients.
Mention the impact or consequences	**SO?** therefore... then... I recommend/conclude...	– Supplying agricultural producers likely violates Ontario regulations and therefore has serious potential to damage Metallo's reputation. (A13) – I conclude that the purchase price of $5,000,000 offered for the common shares is fair.
Explain specifically what to do	**HOW?** how much/many what where when who	– I recommend that data from each location be submitted on a regular (daily) basis to Metallo's head office. (A21) – All acquisitions in excess of $25,000 should be subject to authorization by the comptroller.

EXAMPLES ILLUSTRATING THE DRAFTING STRUCTURE

PROBLEM OR ISSUE	ANALYZE/EVALUATION	RECOMMENDATION/ADVICE (or conclusion)
Internal control weaknesses (AS: Assurance) E.g.: no segregation of duties	DISCUSS the impact of the weaknesses E.g.: The bookkeeper could misappropriate cash by writing-off receivables.	HOW to mitigate the weaknesses E.g.: The responsibility for writing-off the receivables should be transferred to the comptroller.
Accounting treatment of transactions (FA: Financial accounting) E.g.: cost model or revaluation model for buildings (IFRS)	EXPLAIN the application of each of the accounting methods E.g.: According to the revaluation model, buildings could be recorded at their value of $3,000,000 and the depreciation would then be calculated on this increased value.	WHAT is the recommend model E.g.: Based on the needs expressed by the stakeholders to follow the value of the organization, I recommend the revaluation model.
Risks associated with relocating the manufacturing (A5) (BE: Business environment) E.g.: uncertainty of the agriculture market	EXPLAIN impact/cost of the risks E.g.: The relocation of the Liquified product may not be profitable in the long term.	HOW to mitigate the risks E.g.: Conduct a market study in order to determine the existence and size of the market prior to transferring production to Ontario. (A22)
Disclosure of confidential information (ET : Ethics and trust) E.g.: The previous auditor provided a potential purchaser with the financial statements.	EXPLAIN why this is a problem and DESCRIBE the ethical standards E.g.: CEPROC states that a CGA must not reveal confidential information obtained in the course of his duties without proper and specific authority.	WHAT are the steps to follow E.g.: Try to communicate with the CGA colleague. E.g.: Notify the CGA Association of the situation.
Special order required by a client (MA : Management accounting) E.g.: relevant costs to consider	DISCUSS and EXPLAIN which costs are relevant E.g.: The allocation of the overhead costs should not be considered because they are essentially fixed.	CONCLUSION E.g.: Considering only the additional variable costs, the unit cost is $12, which is lower than the offer received of $15.

COMMENT

In order to improve the relevance of the response while facilitating the drafting thereof, it is sometimes appropriate to wonder about the sequencing of the topics. Sometimes there are cause-to-effect relations between the topics and recognizing this facilitates the resolution of the problems or issues.

AJX CASE: Recommending the purchase of the equipment instead of the leasing thereof (A19) will require obtaining long-term financing, which increases the risks associated with relocating (A22).

One can also observe the existence of a natural sequence in the presentation of certain topics. For instance, it is generally preferable to treat the accounting aspect prior to the auditing aspect. In addition, a discussion of an investment usually precedes a discussion of the financing thereof.

The following are a few additional TIPS which will help you to submit relevant ideas:

- *Do not forget to characterize the idea submitted,* if applicable. Is it positive or negative? Is it greater or less? How is it a benefit or disadvantage?

  E.g.: A computerized system will allow one to obtain a **more** timely information for decision-making.

  E.g.: Based on the ratio analysis, your business is financially **very** strong.

- *Do not lose sight of the response plan during the drafting process.* Personally, I regularly reread my reading notes in order not to detract from that which is Required while ensuring that I have an adequate coverage of the problems or issues to be resolved.

  E.g.: Rereading the Required element which asks you to "Address both qualitative and quantitative issues" will remind you not to forget to include in your analysis any appropriate calculations.

COMMENT

A response that purports to be relevant will be drafted with a constant consideration in mind of the case facts. It is, therefore, inappropriate to reinvent or change the case by basing one's response on strict hypotheticals. In other words, one must be careful not to abuse the following expressions: "Yes, but if ...", "Perhaps...", "If one assumes that ... ", etc. It is too easy, by using an "if" or a "perhaps", to deviate from the case parameters. Incidentally, you will note that, in such circumstances, your discussion can be nothing other than general, since it lacks specific support.

Let us assume, for instance, that the Executive Director has asked you to compare the two options considered for the development of the new information system. It would be useless to expatiate on a third possibility which you might conjure up. In the absence of any case fact, you could, at the most, mention this possibility in general terms.

- *Take into account the financial information supplied in the exhibit.* This is often useful in order to justify the importance of a topic or to add quality to an idea.

  E.g.: The control risk is higher due to the fact that the item Inventory adjustments is twice as high as the previous year.

COMMENT

Striking an adequate balance between DEPTH and BREADTH during the drafting process is one of the greatest challenges in the resolution of a case within a restricted time frame. The best manner to improve is to practise by replicating examination conditions. I remind you that you must seek to satisfy the following objectives:

> Responding to that which is Required,
> in light of the particulars of the case
> AND
> Analyzing all the primary problems or issues, and perhaps even
> the topics, that are important as well as part of the others.

Indeed, it may very well be that one can succeed in a case even if one has forgotten or neglected one of the questions asked. Actually, this is quite possible. However, since we do not know to what extent this may be the case, I consider that the above-mentioned drafting strategy should be followed to the extent possible.

  ⦿   *Know how to adapt to circumstances.* Since each case is unique, flexibility and adaptation are required. The objectives to be considered, the decision-making criteria, the manners of proceeding or the characteristics of the situations with which you are faced may be different. For instance, we know that a working capital of more than 1.0 is usually acceptable. However, this is no longer true if the industry averages a ratio of 2.2 or if the bank covenant requires no less than 1.5.

Computations

If applicable, any computations required for a 100 minute case (this is less frequent in a 50 minute case) should be short and precise. They must have their rationale and I suggest that you clearly establish what the purpose of the calculation which you wish to undertake is. Indeed, this will avoid you becoming involved in calculations that are too lengthy or of limited usefulness. For instance, there are four pages of financial information in the exhibits to the AJX CASE. There is no doubt that the challenge consists in only performing the calculations which may be useful to the resolution of the problems or issues.

A calculation is relevant depending on the use that is made thereof.

Most of the required calculations are simple and can be easily incorporated into the body of the response itself, often in brackets. The computation of a ratio or a capital gain, for instance, can be easily added in this manner. If you must make assumptions, I suggest that you set them out clearly and quickly from the outset.

SUGGESTIONS WITH RESPECT TO WORKING ASSUMPTIONS

The assumptions to mention in this response are those that are derived from a choice.	If the case mentions, for instance, that the marginal tax rate is 40%, one must use this rate. There is no need to explain its origin in the list of assumptions. On the other hand, if no rate is mentioned, you will be required to justify the one you will have selected.
The assumptions selected must be realistic, reasonable and easy to work with.	One must exercise judgment in determining the shelf life of a product or the duration of a project. Deciding on 10 years although the product is one that becomes rapidly obsolete is unrealistic. On the other hand, one must exercise prudence in the determination of the future revenues set out in the budget, by selecting the median between the optimistic scenario and the pessimistic scenario. N.B.: Without any case facts, it would be useless, for instance, to become burdened down by an inflation rate of 2%.
The assumptions must be based on the data provided in the case.	If the case mentions that the variable manufacturing expenses are equal to 50% of the direct labour costs, it would be pointless to change this fact by making a different and arbitrary assumption. Barring any notice to the contrary, the information supplied in the case is accurate and may be used as such.

COMMENT

I suggest that you develop the reflex of ensuring the likelihood of a computation you have performed before using it. It is too easy to perform a calculation and then to transition into the qualitative analysis without ensuring that the result obtained is likely. I suggest, therefore, that you take a few seconds to ask yourself if the computation you have just performed makes sense.

AJX CASE: Assume you have obtained a gross margin of 64% for the liquified product. This clearly does not make sense when you take a quick look at the figures set out in the case. Validating the result obtained may, therefore, spare you the drafting of a biased analysis just because you typed one "0" too many!

Integrated ideas

One must constantly keep in mind the objective of writing a response which is integrated with the particulars of the case. Each response is unique since each case is. In other words, you must call upon your baggage of theoretical knowledge in the resolution of the various problems or issues specific to your employer or your client. Your response must, therefore, apply to the organization under study and not to all organizations generally. For instance, stating "that it is important to have accurate reports on the various functions and duties within the organization" is not bad, but it is general in nature. It is far preferable, for instance, to designate the "production" function or the "sales" function since these are referred to in the case.

In order to be in a position to identify what aspects your discussion will bear upon, you must, therefore, fully understand the theoretical concepts of the topics under study. This is crucial. It is not appropriate to write all that you know on a topic without exercising any judgment.

In order to demonstrate your professional abilities, you must aim for the **simultaneous integration of theory and practice**. Most of the time, this will occur in the same sentence or in the same paragraph.

Here are a few examples of ideas that are adequately integrated, that is to say that they refer both to theoretical concepts (in green) and to case facts (in yellow).

- ℭ I recommend considering each branch as a profit centre and not as a revenue centre, since the manager has the necessary authority in order to approve the expenses.

- ℭ AJX CASE: These are integrated foreign operations since AJX/Metallo monitor the decisions and activities. I conclude that one must use the temporal method.

- ℭ Due to the fact that certain journal entries were passed with no supporting documents, one will have to pay greater attention to "occurrence" and "existence" assertions during the inventory audit.

As illustrated by the examples above, one must call upon useful theoretical concepts in the resolution of a problem or issue. For instance, discussing the existence of an investment centre as a responsibility centre would not be relevant if the branches referred to in the case do not have any investments.

> **COMMENT**
>
> Case integration is a difficult competency to acquire. Instead, candidates tend to set out all the theoretical concepts they know, and then present what is applicable to the case in the following paragraph. One must make a true effort to demonstrate that one knows exactly what the organization needs.

Indeed, it sometimes occurs that the Required elements of a case direct you towards the presentation of a summary of the theoretical concepts on a given topic. For instance, the shareholders could ask you to explain to them what the duties and responsibilities of an audit committee are. Make no mistake about it, you should reply to this type of request, which is usually directed, if not explicit. However, I suggest that you seek out the reason or context for this request – and no doubt there is one set out in the case – in order to perfect the quality of your response. Hence, you might discover that the shareholders plan to go public next year. You could also use the particulars of the organization or of its environment in order to illustrate some of your ideas, for instance, the fact that the internal controls must be improved.

> **COMMENT**
>
> When you draft a case, try and visualize what is going on in order to better understand the particulars. In the heat of the action, it is unfortunately often the case that candidates will write ideas that are not very realistic. Use your practical sense and make analogies with what you already know. For instance, knowing that medication has an expiry date, pay attention to case facts with respect to the inventory turnover. Also, use caution when your client, who is 61 years old, and likely close to retiring and probably risk averse, asks for your advice on his investments.

Here are two additional TIPS which will assist you in presenting integrated ideas:

- Use the names of the protagonists in the case, of the organization (abbreviated, as AJX) or of its products. Personalize your statements by directing them to the appropriate person. Feeling closer to the case promotes integration.

  AJX CASE: I recommend examining in greater detail why the gross margin of the liquified product is much lower than that of other products.

- Use brackets wisely. At times, this allows you to present case integration with greater efficiency.

  E.g.: All fixed costs (rent, selling, administrative) are excluded from the calculation of the marginal contribution in order to determine if the price offered for this special order covers direct costs.

Useful recommendations and conclusions

It is generally recognized that a structured method for the resolution of a problem or issue leads to a recommendation or a conclusion. This finality of any analysis is essential since it demonstrates that you are exercising professional judgment.

Here are a few tips with respect to recommendations and conclusions:

- *Make sure that the recommendation does indeed resolve the problem raised.* The relationship must be direct. "A suggestion that employees be provided with training" is a good idea if their lack of knowledge is the problem. However, if the problem is instead the lack of integration of information between the inventory system and the accounting system, training employees will not be a relevant recommendation.

- As often as possible, *start your recommendations by using a verb in the infinitive or an imperative.* Hence, you avoid uselessly watering down what you are stating, out of a fear of being wrong. The words "MUST" or "SHOULD" are generally preferable to the words "could" or "would".

EXAMPLE (NOT RECOMMENDED)

Further to the analysis above, I could recommend that you develop a custom-built software system or purchase an off-the-shelf system.

N.B.: No position is taken here. Instead, further to the analysis, one must clearly set out one's opinion or recommendation, with confidence, and accept responsibility for one's proposal.

EXAMPLE (RECOMMENDED)

I recommend that you develop a custom-built system <u>since</u> your employees possess the necessary expertise.

COMMENT

I remind you that there is usually more than one valid solution for a given problem or issue. The important thing is that your recommendation is adequate and supported by the analysis.

✠ *Determine specifically the action to be taken;* say WHAT MUST BE DONE and WHY in precise and concrete terms. The person receiving the instructions must easily understand what you want to say. Writing, for instance, "approvals are needed" is not sufficiently complete. "For what?, "How much?" or "Who?". Also note that recommendations are often simpler than you think.

EXAMPLE (NOT RECOMMENDED)

> I recommend that you exercise greater supervision over how money received by way of donations is spent.
>
> N.B.: This recommendation is general in nature, and not sufficiently tied into the case. In point of fact, it is more or less valid as such for any non-profit organization.

COMMENT

When time comes to conclude the analysis by setting out a recommendation or a conclusion, I take advantage of the opportunity to ask myself if there are any interrelations with other topics. For instance, when I make a recommendation to develop a custom-built system, I can see an opportunity to tie that in with the preceding analysis with respect to the need for timely and reliable financial information. Hence, I can improve my analysis by short sentences which demonstrate my ability to develop an integrative response.

✠ *Adopt a position in a positive and constructive manner.* One must not only criticize the current state of affairs, one must solve the outstanding problems. Stating that "sales transactions are not translated at the proper rate" is not the same as saying "sales must be converted at the exchange rate applicable when the transaction takes place". Finally, failing to make a recommendation due to a lack of information is rarely a good idea.

EXAMPLE (NOT RECOMMENDED)

> Since I do not know the exact amount of the loss incurred as a result of the fire which swept through the Charlottetown branch, I am unable to explain to you how the insurance claim will be accounted for.
>
> N.B.: Do I even need to comment?

COMMENT

Where calculations have been performed, one must ensure that they are adequately interpreted. You must give your opinion and not only repeat in words the result obtained. Also note that a calculation ALWAYS forms part of a qualitative analysis.

AJX CASE: Stating that "The gross margin of the Liquified product is 6.4%." is of little use since the calculation already shows it. One should instead state that "The Liquified product is the least profitable". (A24)

Part 4
Presenting One's Ideas Efficiently

Value-added ideas
Adequate writing style
Appropriate attitudes

"When writing responses,
the challenge is to use concise and complete sentences."

Deslauriers, Sylvie, *Accounting for Success The Guide to Case Resolution*,
AB + Publications, 2010, p. 125.

PART 4
Presenting One's Ideas Efficiently

Drafting a report or a letter which will be the most useful possible for the recipient, whether this be an employer or a client, is the objective to be achieved. In practice, you usually have sufficient time to enhance your report, reread it and improve it. The same does not go for a resolution of a case in a limited time frame. Therefore, you must make your drafting more efficient, and highlight your ideas, in order to maximize your success.

Value-added ideas

Presenting New Ideas. Basically, the employer or the client expects the CGA accounting professional to present it/him/her with value-added ideas. In other words, your response must contain ideas which the intended audience of the report does not know. An idea is new if it has not previously been set forth in the case or in the preceding pages of your response. Assume, for instance, that your employer is seeking solutions in order to motivate his or her employees and is considering a "bonus package plan based on residual income". Since the idea originates from him or her, you will have to go further than simply repeating the idea, you will have to discuss it. On the other hand, if your employer has not considered this solution, suggesting this idea will have value in and of itself.

AJX CASE

The board of directors asks Megan to assist with two issues: Divisional structure and Financial statement audit. We observe that all information regarding the Current Issues originates from the board of directors. Since the letter which Megan is required to write under a. is specifically directed to the members of the board, it would be useless to summarize, for instance, what the relocation plan for the three sales divisions is all about. When you approach the resolution of the case, you must start from the premise that the recipient of the report knows the information that he or she has forwarded to you. In b., one must acknowledge that John does not have all the information that Megan possesses. Indeed, he has received the nonconsolidated, unaudited financial statements of Metallo (Exhibit 4-2), along with the three divisional income statements (Exhibits 4-3, 4-4, 4-5) (A5). Since he is not aware, for instance, of the relocation plan for the three sales divisions, he can quite simply not discuss it in his letter. He will, however, consider that the board of directors knows the financial information presented in the exhibits which Megan forwarded to him.

**One must draft one's response in
simple, clear, precise and concrete terms.**

COMMENT

It is not infrequent that candidates will summarize the case before beginning to resolve it. This is a waste of time. Some candidates wrongly believe, in such a case, that they have drafted a response of sufficient depth. When the idea is not new, it is quite simply not taken into account in the assessment of the response.

Of course, one must understand what is going on in the organization before beginning to resolve a problem or issue. This is an undeniable fact, but this process can take place mentally, and should not uselessly waste your time. Under certain circumstances, where the situation does not appear to you to be clear, it is possible to proceed with a summarization on a worksheet.

EXAMPLE (NOT RECOMMENDED)

> You tell me that you have adopted a bonus package plan based on residual income five years ago. You deemed it to be sufficient and responsible for the proper performance of your organization. However, you have observed a decrease in motivation among your employees and you are asking me to find some solutions. Further to my analysis, here is what I suggest:

This summary of the information contained in the case is useless, since it includes no new idea, or even a relevant one. Allow me to remind you that you must use the time allotted to you optimally with a view to the resolution of the case. Regarding the example set out above, a clear and precise title is sufficient to situate the reader, and enables you to approach the "analysis" of your report in quicker fashion. You will understand that the use of titles and subtitles guides efficient drafting.

EXAMPLE (RECOMMENDED)

> Decrease in motivation of employees:

COMMENT

It may happen that the information supplied in the case was compiled by you directly further to observations or meetings with employees, for instance. It may also consist of information originating from external sources, such as a series of ratios from the industry, for instance.

In these situations, the intended audience is not necessarily aware of the information in question. You must take this into account in your manner of drafting, without, however, launching into the drafting of a long and useless summary.

Use the Case Facts. Case facts serve to justify, explain, criticize, describe, assess or recommend the new ideas which you are submitting. Case facts are "incidentals" which enable you to provide a better response. Taken individually, they do not provide the response in and of itself. Used adequately, they contribute to demonstrating your integration capacity, as illustrated by the examples set out in Part 3, page 28.

Diversifying the Ideas Submitted. In order to obtain a satisfactory response to a case, one must write quite a few different, relevant and new ideas with respect to a certain number of problems or issues. As mentioned previously, one must attempt to deal with all the primary problems or issues (important) and part of the others.

COMMENT

It is often said that the ideas that are the most accessible on a topic appear in the first few minutes of one's analysis. The greater number of simulations you engage in, the more you will hone your capacity to react quickly. When one begins to resolve cases, one hesitates or often searches for what to say. As you acquire experience, the challenge becomes choosing instead which ideas to write on a specific topic before going on to the next.

This challenge is particularly difficult for perfectionists, hence the importance of having prepared a response plan that guides the drafting phase. It is generally better to go on to the next important problem than to perfect the analysis of the current problem by adding details. The last few minutes spent on a topic are often less productive than the first few minutes devoted to the following topic.

Avoid Repeating the Same Ideas. Certain candidates repeat the same thing, sometimes using other words, thereby wasting time. It is useless to repeat, for instance, the same idea both in the analysis and in the recommendation.

EXAMPLE (NOT RECOMMENDED)

> In the determination of your dividend policy, one must consider that the organization needs to retain its liquidities for investment in the United States.
>
> I recommend that you retain the same dividend payout ratio as the previous year, because the organization needs to retain its liquidities for investment in the United States.

I suggest that you diversify your arguments. Suggesting, for instance, that a specialist be hired as an audit procedure for each of the assets in the balance sheet is not a good idea. One must diversify the procedures. If a specialist is required in more than one sector – which is rare – one can then group the ideas instead of repeating them. Also, for instance, if the case asks you to discuss the accounting treatment of two new investments, rest assured that they probably do not require the same accounting treatment. One of the objectives of learning according to the case method is to enable you to demonstrate your knowledge. You will certainly not be required to repeat the same concepts for two different investments.

COMMENT

It is clearly pointless to repeat the same ideas, since that they will only be considered once in the assessment of the response. However, I wish to remind you that it is quite possible that a single case fact will be used in more than one problem or issue. A single topic can also be approached in various contexts.

AJX CASE: You are required to discuss the accounting AND tax treatment of the intercompany transactions (A11, A12).

Give Precedence to Substance Over Form. Never lose sight of this fundamental accounting principle. It is the quality of the ideas written in your solution that will count, and not the manner in which you present them. While the presentation of ideas in an appropriate format is a competency which you must demonstrate, you must do so with efficiency. Certain candidates give it so much importance that they lack time to draft a QUALITY response, which also sets out a sufficient QUANTITY of ideas. In addition, I could add that a great quantity of ideas, although a minimum is necessary, does not compensate for a lack of quality.

Trust in Yourself. You should not waste time asking yourself if it is relevant to write such and such an idea. Some candidates are so afraid of making a mistake or looking stupid before an assessor that they refrain from writing ideas which ultimately turn out to be adequate. Obviously, you can spend some time planning a response, but the limited time frame afforded to you in a case does not allow for hesitation.

> **COMMENT**
>
> There is usually no negative marking in the assessment of a response. A somewhat stupid idea, or even one that is outright false, does not invalidate the rest. Under stress, this is comprehensible, and you must know that the assessors have seen other blunders. It also happens that a candidate will discuss a problem or issue which is irrelevant and, therefore, does not contribute to the success of the case. The main damage caused is the waste of time that ensues, but it does not alter the assessment of the rest of the response.
>
> However, one must pay attention not to contradict one's own statements. If you do so, your ideas cancel out and will appropriately not be considered in the assessment.

Adequate writing style

With a view to presenting your response to a case in the most efficient manner possible, here are a series of TIPS:

- *Use Ink.* Writing is faster, which simply enables you to write a greater amount of ideas in the same time frame. It is pointless to waste your time embellishing the text by using different colours or underlining. The assessor does not need you to indicate what your best ideas are in order to take them into account. And ... please do not write in red!

  If you made a mistake, do not cross the information out, simply place the text or the calculation between brackets and write "draft" next to it. Do not start again from the beginning! There is perhaps something good in what you are about to delete.

- *Use Titles and Subtitles.* In this manner, you avoid summarizing the case or adding an introduction to your analysis. With an adequate title, the intended recipient of your report is clearly oriented. In addition, and this is not a benefit which is to be underestimated, this forces you to specify that which you wish to discuss. Clearly establishing from the outset what the problem or issue to be solved is resolutely turns your discussion towards that which is essential. Also highlight your opinions, recommendations and conclusions by including an appropriate reference.

◎ *Spread Your Text Across the Page.* If your handwriting is difficult to read, skip a line between each written line. Start each primary problem or issue on a new page in order to be able to add an idea, if need be.

Present your calculations in such a manner that the assessor will know where your result come from. Very short explanations are sufficient, there is no need to explain the origin of the figures which are taken directly from the case. The list of assumptions, if any, must be succinct; no more than one line or two per assumption. Where the calculation is too long in order to be placed in brackets in the text, one should present it on a separate page to which one refers. The purpose of the calculation, as well as a brief conclusion, then appear on the schedule. Do not hesitate to round your figures out where the circumstances allow.

◎ *Opt for an Appropriate Abbreviated Style.* The challenge consists in writing sentences that are both complete and concise. Certain candidates take too much time to write their ideas. Their response then appears in the form of long paragraphs which contain an insufficient number of different ideas. Conversely, the text is so abbreviated that it is difficult to understand the proposal put forth. The recipient of the report – and under the circumstances, the assessor – must understand that which is written without having to ask questions or add words.

If a candidate wishes to show an interrelation between two topics, he or she must write it. One should not expect the assessor to "deduce" that this link exists simply because the two topics are discussed in the paragraphs that follow each other or appear on the same page.

DRAFTING IN A STYLE THAT IS TOO ABBREVIATED (NOT RECOMMENDED)

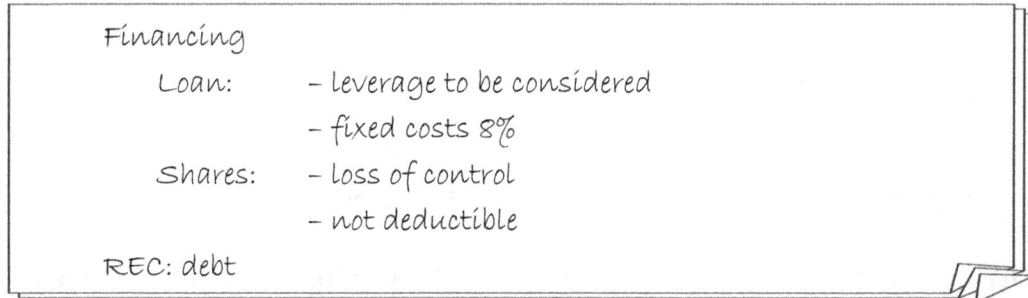

```
Financing
   Loan:      – leverage to be considered
              – fixed costs 8%
   Shares:    – loss of control
              – not deductible
REC: debt
```

The previous example clearly highlights the fact that words are missing. What is to be considered with the "leverage"? In this case, one cannot even tell if it is a benefit or a disadvantage, since it is not specified. Same thing for "fixed costs". Loss of control? It is a general idea that no doubt could be complemented by a case fact. Indeed, this response seems adapted to any organization asking itself if it should opt for a financing by way of loan or by issuance of shares. What is "not deductible"? The shares? The dividends? It must be specified. Indeed, I suspect that the candidate is referring to the dividends, however I cannot assume that which has not been said. An assessor reads that which is written, black on white. He or she has no obligation to add words or to determine what the candidate probably wished to say. The assessment of a response is an objective process. Finally, the recommendation should ALWAYS be substantiated, if possible using a different argument from those set out in the previous analysis.

DRAFTING STYLE NOT SUFFICIENTLY ABBREVIATED (NOT RECOMMENDED)

> Financing by loan from the bank or by issuing new shares
>
> You are asking if it is preferable to finance the new project by way of loan or by the issuance of new shares. This is my thinking on the issue:
>
> When you borrow, you can take advantage of what we refer to in finance as "leverage". Leverage is an amplification of the return on equity when the return on assets exceeds the interest on debt. This is because interest paid represents fixed costs. In your situation, XYZ would receive a leverage, since the cost of financing of 8% is far less than the profitability anticipated for the project of 12%.

The previous example clearly demonstrates that it is easy to waste time drafting a text, which, although this well written, is uselessly long. We will note here that we have only broached the first argument – the first idea – in favour of financing by way of loan. The theoretical expatiation on leverage is of little usefulness for a client. Instead, one should directly apply the notions to the particulars of the case, in a language which the intended recipient will understand. Finally, note that the introduction to the topic is useless, and that it repeats the title.

ADEQUATE WRITING STYLE (RECOMMENDED)

> Financing by loan or shares
>
> By opting for financing by way of loan, XYZ would be able to take advantage of a leverage effect since the cost of the financing of 8% is by far less than the anticipated profitability of the project of 12%. The interest will be tax deductible. However, this is a fixed cost which becomes a recurrent cash outflow.
>
> By issuing new shares, you risk losing control, since you currently hold 55% of XYZ. In addition, the dividends which may be paid will not be tax deductible.
>
> I recommend debt financing, since the cash inflows of the project will be sufficient to cover the outflow of the repayment thereof.

The previous example is a model to follow. The title orients the discussion. Each sentence is complete: one subject, one verb, one object. The meaning of the idea, namely whether it is a benefit or a disadvantage, is clear. The structure is efficient: one paragraph with respect to financing by way of loan and a paragraph with respect to the issuance of shares. The recommendation is supported by the analysis. The theoretical notions (in green) are well integrated with the case facts (in yellow).

One idea → One complete sentence

38

> **COMMENT**
>
> There are circumstances where it is possible to present the text in a more abbreviated fashion, where one is required to list a series of items having a common thread, namely a "LIST OF".
>
> Examples:
> - audit procedures to be performed;
> - advantages and disadvantages of going public;
> - items to disclose in the related party transactions note to the financial statements (A14);
> - what can be done to reduce audit fees;
> - additional information to obtain.
>
> One could also abbreviate further the explanations or the items surrounding the calculations

☺ ***Use Professional Language;*** i.e. business language. In other words, NO JARGON. You should banish expressions or words from the vernacular whose meaning is not clear. For instance, stating that "The previous auditor took short cuts in the work he performed on the inventory" is unspecific. One should state instead: "The previous auditor did not ensure that inventory was measured at the lower of cost and net realizable value, since …".

It is, however, possible to use abbreviations in your response; abbreviations which must be easy to recognize by your colleagues. Indeed, the assessor of your response must certainly not ask himself or herself what you mean to say. Under certain circumstances, when you know you are going to regularly repeat a certain expression, you can indicate an abbreviation when you use it the first time. E.g.: Disaster Recovery Plan (DRP).

The following is a non-exhaustive list of abbreviations that are generally recognized:

MIS	Management Information System	ACB	Adjusted Cose Base
BOD	Board of Directors	NPV	Net present Value
FMV	Fair Market Value	COGS	Cost of Good Solds

☺ ***Use a Simple Drafting Style.*** Your text does not need to be written in impeccable English. If you use the words "superior" twice in the same sentence, for instance, it does not matter. The objective is to present one's ideas clearly. Therefore, I suggest that you opt for a simple style in respect of the tenses of the verbs. Specifically, the present tense, the past perfect or the future tense are to be preferred. Nothing complicated.

One should pay relative attention to grammar and the spelling. Indeed, if you make more mistakes than the average person or if these mistakes render your text incomprehensible, you must make some efforts in this area. Otherwise, do not be overly bothered by this aspect and concentrate your efforts instead on the drafting of relevant and new ideas.

⟲ *Be Positive and Constructive.* The employer or client is asking you for assistance in resolving its/his/her problems or issues. Hence, you must conduct your analyses in such a manner that they will lead to useful and concrete solutions. It is preferable to say what should be done as opposed as to what should not be done. Of course, one must regularly explain why such a problem exists or why such an issue is important. It is, however, the first step towards the resolution of this problem or issue. For instance, recognizing that there exists a "conflict of interest for John to work on the audit of Metallo" is only the first step; one must thereafter analyze what the consequences thereof are, in order to ultimately recommend concrete actions such as "John must remove himself from the audit": this is the proper manner of proceeding. (A31)

Finally, note that an interrogatory style is not truly in your best interests. E.g.: "Should I remove myself from the audit?" This sentence does not clearly take position. Yet, your role is to answer questions, not to ask them!

Appropriate attitudes

In order to guide you in the drafting of your response to a case, I wish to introduce you to certain attitudes (whether implicit or explicit) which will influence the drafting of your ideas.

Play a leading role

As a CGA professional accountant, you are the main contact for your employer or your client. By showing your competency and your objectivity, you are the only person able to identify what is wrong or needs to be changed, to analyze the problems or issues, and ultimately recommend solutions. For instance, one must not tell oneself that the audit partner knows full well what procedures to perform and pursuant to what assertion, and then move on to something else. If the Required elements ask you to supply a list of procedures, do so. Similarly, if you are asked to discuss risks associated with relocating (A5), and you observe that the profitability of the products varies greatly from one product to the next, you should raise the issue. You cannot simply ignore this issue just because Metallo is held by a public company which monitors the decisions and activities of all its subsidiaries (A2). Where the case facts are present, you must play a lead role and resolve all the problems or issues.

Write your response for the benefit of a non-management employee

The recipient of your report must understand what you are saying without having to ask you questions or make assumptions. In order to assist the candidates whom I am supervising, I suggest that they pretend they are directing their comments to a non-management employee. This employee has the ability to do that which you ask, however the instructions must be clear and precise. For instance, telling him to "do audit work on the Land item" is too vague. Instead, you should tell him "To ensure the occurrence of the new land, you need to examine the acquisition contract". What someone should do and why should be indicated. You are not required to explain the basic concepts of our field, such as debit = credit, however your statements must be clear and explicit.

Comply with the business policies of an employer or client

One should never lose sight of the fact that one is working for an employer or a client in order to resolve problems or issues that are specific to the latter. In point of fact, one must consider the objectives, needs, preferences and bias of stakeholders, without bringing any judgment to bear on these aspects. Through the position that we take, we must take into account these items, without overly upsetting the manners of thinking or of doing. For instance, we know that AJX's management and board of directors monitor the decisions and activities of all of its subsidiaries (A2). We must not question that fact, unless, of course, you are being asked your opinion on the topic.

Our role is to remain objective, and our personal, social, political or human opinions must not interfere with our analyses.

Consider the monetary aspect of the events

As mentioned in Part 3, one must identify and use the financial data supplied in the case as part of the analysis of the various problems or issues. What I would like to add is that the monetary aspect of the events is a consideration that pervades any response. In other words, one must regularly refer to the financial consequences, even in the absence of any figures. For instance, the impact of a weakness in the inventory internal control will be expressed taking into account the carrying costs. Similarly, lack of compliance with regulations may indeed have an impact on public health, but could also lead to legal costs or a drop in sales (A20, A22).

Be Honest

In our profession, it is essential to exhibit ethical behaviour or to act in a moral manner. Therefore, it is essential to follow the word and spirit of the CGA *Code of Ethical Principles and Rules of Conduct*. A professional accountant complies with legislation, does not in any way become associated with fraudulent transactions and must undertake the necessary steps where a colleague has not acted appropriately. He or she also has a duty to notify the employer or the client of the consequences of any action taken. For instance, the client should be told that the personal benefits that he or she is deriving from his or her company must be recorded on his or her T4 or that producing potentially hazardous materials subjects him or her to liability for public health (A13).

Being honest is also knowing one's limits. As a newly-certified CGA, you cannot be specialized in fields requiring great expertise, such as international tax issues (A26). Therefore, you must on occasion call upon a specialist, such as in the case of the assessment of built-in machinery.

Show respect

One should be careful, that is to say that one should weigh the use of one's words, when speaking of individuals, in particular of one's colleagues. One must state that which needs to be stated, however using diplomacy. In certain cases, it is a regular occurrence to notice errors on the part of employees, such as the consideration of sunk costs in a net present value calculation. One must identify the mistake, and correct it, but be careful not to issue drastic judgments with respect to people. It is generally preferable to "suggest a course of training" rather than to "dismiss a person for incompetence". Personally, I prefer to speak of written reports or actions taken by individuals rather than refer to the individuals themselves. One must also be cautious in fraud situations. On the one hand, one must not confuse incompetence and fraud. On the other hand, we are entitled to "suspect" a fraud, but not to state that it exists as a *fait accompli*.

Part 5
Analyzing the Suggested Solution and the Competency Grids

The Suggested Solution
Competency Grids
The Things to Remember

"CGAs possess a wide range of cross-functional knowledge and skills,
which enhances their ability to take a value-added,
integrative approach to solving complex business problems."

CGA Competency framework, CGA-Canada, 2010, p. 13.

PART 5

Analyzing the Suggested Solution and the Competency Grids

I deem it essential to take the time to analyze the suggested solution and the Competency Grids as soon as possible after the simulation of a case. As you will observe below, the process involves not only reading, but analyzing. Personally, in a practice exam case, I devote approximately twice the time allotted for the case to this analysis. For a 100 minute case, for instance, it takes me between two and a half hours to three hours.

> **COMMENT**
>
> This part includes many tricks and tips aimed at helping you in the analysis of the suggested solution and of the Competency Grids. The ultimate goal is to understand the manner in which the resolution of the case is built and assessed.
>
> I very often meet candidates who criticize the case, its resolution or the grid. In my opinion, this is not a very good attitude. It is much more constructive and useful to seek to understand HOW and WHY things are the way they are. There is always an explanation and finding it will help you develop your competency in the resolution of the cases.

The Suggested Solution[1]

Highlighting the Structure of the Solution

From the outset, one must examine the structure of the suggested solution, namely the response plan, with a view to identifying all the problems or issues. One must draw up a list of the topics presented and indicate to which part(s) of the Required elements they relate. Personally, where the text is written in an uninterrupted format, I write titles and subtitles in the solution.

Highlighting the structure of the solution allows me to take stock of the following items:

- *Depth of the Discussion.* The objective is to determine which are the problems or issues that are the most important. After the fact, one can compare what one has observed with the prioritization of the topics which was established during the simulation of the case.

    AJX CASE: The Required element "make recommendations on reporting periods for subsidiaries" is a less important issue than the others (A12).

- *Sequencing of Topics.* The objective is to determine if the discussion of the topic must precede that of another. One could observe, for instance, that one must recompute the net income prior to discussing the bonus payable to the President.

- *Steps Followed in the Resolution of a Problem or Issue.* The objective is to understand the logic underlying the discussion.

    AJX CASE: In the analysis of the items to be reviewed in order to produce Metallo's financial statements in compliance with the IFRS, one presents similarities AND differences. Greater focus is afforded to the latter (A14, A15).

- *Manner of Presenting Topics.* The objective is to spot those areas where part of the solution is presented in the form of a list or a table.

---

[1] The manner of analyzing the suggested solution is amply illustrated by the AJX case (A11 to A15).

Review the Case Parameters

All throughout the reading of the proposed solution, I suggest that you regularly return to the case parameters: the Required elements, the Role and the Context. Hence, one must, at least *ex post facto*, ensure that one understands all the particulars of the case. It may be, for example, that you did not see the significance of the fact that AJX was operating in a "regulated environment" (A13). When you take cognizance of that fact by reading the solution, you must then return to the case to identify the case facts that escaped your attention (A4).

The presence of problems or issues, as well as their significance, must be explained. If you did not see a request or you improperly assessed the significance thereof, you must seek out how you could have avoided making this mistake.

AJX CASE (A5)

It may be, for instance, that one observes, after the fact, that the applicable financial reporting framework to be used is not the same under a. and under b. Under a., the discussion essentially refers to the accounting standards currently followed by Metallo, namely the Accounting Standards for Private Enterprises (ASPE). It is under b. that the Required elements request that you review the financial statements in accordance with IFRS. You must, therefore, use the adequate framework, at the proper place.

Understanding the Ideas Contained in the Solution

I suggest that you take advantage of the opportunity you are given to perfect your knowledge. Each idea, each argument and each calculation must be understood, regardless of their importance in the case. A secondary issue in this case may well become a primary issue in the following case. Here, the objective is to understand the theoretical concepts put forth, which, quite often, means returning to your reference volumes. Upon reading the suggested solution, you could notice, for instance, that you need to refresh your knowledge on the topic of Foreign currency translation.

Personally, I also take the opportunity to identify the cause-to-effect links or connections between the various topics.

**One must grasp the theoretical knowledge in the program
to write a professional application exam.**

Tying the Solution to the Case Facts

When carefully reading the suggested solution, you must constantly pay attention to the fact that it arises directly from the case. This is not a fortuitous event. Each idea comprising the solution is there for a reason, in light of the Required elements. The ties between the case facts and their resolution are cast in stone and, as often as possible, they must be fleshed out. This means that you will surely and regularly return to read the case in order to explain the solution. The more often you will conduct this exercise, the more revealing the reading of the next case will appear to you to be.

EXAMPLES EXPLAINING THE PRESENCE OF AN IDEA
WITHIN THE PROPOSED SOLUTION USING CASE FACTS.

Component of the suggested solution	Case fact
As part of the Required element "discuss how to improve cash flow and financial results", a discussion of the various means available in order to mitigate the foreign exchange risk is presented.	"Sales to customers outside Canada had greatly increased during the year and this tendency opts to continue in the future".
The potential acquisition of new equipment is an example in the accounting discussion on foreign currency translation (A11).	"Metallo would need to invest in new equipment for the Ontario location..." (A4)
As part of the Required element "address the issues of concern", a discussion of the tax consequences of not paying a bonus within 180 days is presented.	"The financial statements show that a Bonus payable to the President of $55,000. Is in the balance sheet (statement of financial position) since 2 years."

Study the Integration of the Theoretical Concepts With the Case Facts

I strongly suggest that you pay particular attention to the selection of theoretical concepts used in the solution, as well as to their integration to the case data.

> AJX CASE (A11)
>
> In preparing the consolidated statements, it will be important that all intercompany transactions between Metallo and its subsidiaries be tracked and eliminated (for example, the potential loan from Metallo to a Mexican subsidiary) and only transactions with external entities remain.

In the above example, the theoretical concepts (in green) which are necessary to the discussion are clearly set out and explained in connection with the case facts (in yellow). This manner of proceeding allows for a quicker analysis of the contents of the solution. Also note the efficient use of brackets.

In addition to the above, I frequently take a step back and highlight a key concept in the resolution of the problem or issue. Thus, one can identify the fact that the "cost/benefit concept" underlies the analysis (A13).

Fleshing Out the Relevant Ideas

All throughout the reading of the solution, I annotate the ideas that I am reading in such a manner as to highlight the key items raised. For instance, I may represent part of the text by a diagram (A11) or summarize the theory in the form of a table (A12). I write "ST" (short term) and "LT" (long term) in order to indicate that the temporal horizon has been considered. Otherwise, I number the steps or alternatives. Finally, I regularly point out the following items:

ⓒ The ideas that answer the questions WHY? SO? HOW? (Part 3, page 23). This highlights the fact more clearly, for instance, that the ideas must be justified. Furthermore, the impact ("I") of the items observed can be stated. It is sometimes the case as well that the terms WHO, WHEN and WHERE will be useful, where the discussion bears on the internal control, for example.

ⓒ The recommendations, opinions and conclusions. This fleshes out the actions to be taken ("R" or "REC") in order to resolve a given problem or issue. Also, this allows one to observe, for instance, the presence of a firm conclusion to the effect that the previous auditor was in a conflict of interest position.

COMMENT

One can state that the suggested solution to a case is generally a very good solution. The resolution of the principal problems or issues is usually sufficiently complete, in an impeccable structure. I would venture to say that it is a nearly perfect solution, which meets the "Exceeds" level for a majority of competencies. It is a model to be followed as to the number of ideas to write or the degree of depth which a problem or issue may reach.

In point of fact, the resolution of a case in a limited time frame is not as simple. One or several case facts may have escaped your attention, you may have wrongly understood one of the requests or poorly prioritized the problems or issues. It is normal to do so. The purpose I am seeking by explaining to you how to analyze the suggested solution – and, potentially, the Competency Grids – is to help you minimize this type of mistake.

It is not necessary to present a perfect response to succeed in a case. One must, however, constantly strive for this perfection.

Competency Grids[1]

From the outset, I would like to state that a good many of the tips set out previously in the analysis of the suggested solution also apply when time comes to analyze the Competency Grids. Personally, I comment the grids in detail in order to flesh out the particulars.

Inventory of the Competencies Assessed

First of all, I suggest that one take cognizance of the competencies assessed in the case. Some are clearly predictable, whereas others are less obvious, especially where there are non-directed questions. I can tell you from experience that there are always one or two that you have not anticipated and others that will not have the time to consider. You will need to attempt to understand why a little later.

Personally, I focus from the outset on the core and core-related competencies since I consider that they need to be properly understood prior to assessing the professional qualities and skills competencies.

---

1 The manner of analyzing the Competency Grids is amply illustrated by the AJX case (A16 to A32).

> **COMMENT**
>
> I fully understand the fact that a candidate would want to assess his or her response as soon as possible. In point of fact, I often see candidates who do not even take the time to read the suggested solution and instead go directly to identify the performance level obtained for the various competencies which they tackled in their response.
>
> You will understand that I prefer an analysis of the solution and of the grid prior to marking you. On the one hand, this approach is essential to an improvement of the performance since all competencies, whether they have been well or poorly performed, are analyzed. And, on the other hand, knowing the guide well enables one to conduct a fairer and more complete assessment.

Establishing the Relation Between the Guide, the Case and its Solution

It is crucial to justify the presence of each of the competencies in the Competency Grids. Each of them is there for a reason and I recommend that you make the effort of retracing in the case the place where the resolution of each problem or issue is Required. Conversely, I make sure to retrace each of the questions of the Required elements in the solution key for one or several of the competencies.

In the analysis of the Competency Grids, it is regularly useful to review the suggested solution in order to better understand an argument or to be able to identify an "Other valid point". Personally, in respect of each competency, I identify the Required elements as well as the reference page to the suggested solution.

AJX CASE

When establishing the relation between the Competency Grids and the suggested solution, one observes that the solution does not broach the following topic: Review of client information before the engagement is accepted (A28). It does happen, as in the AJX case, that one observes the absence of a secondary issue. One must also recall that it is not necessary to achieve the "Meets" level with respect to all the competencies in the Competency Grids in order to succeed in a case, or to pass a professional examination. However, one must seek to demonstrate one's competency for the greatest number of possible opportunities.

N.B.: The PA1 examination has a particular focus on Financial accounting, Taxation and Assurance. The PA2 examination has a particular focus on Financial accounting, Management accounting and Finance.

Detailed Analysis of the Competency Grids

I suggest that you take time to analyze the components of the Competency Grids in detail. A cursory reading or a singular focus on the performance level that you have achieved is insufficient. One must parse the contents of the solution keys in order to understand the foundations of the assessment. A good comprehension of how this is achieved enables you to improve the quality of your drafting for the next case. Personally, I take the time to flesh out the ties to the case, as well as the interrelations between the topics, if any.

ANALYSIS OF THE CONTENTS OF THE COMPETENCY GRIDS

Analytical objective	Examples of observations
Read the baseline question This question refers to that which is essential in order to be successful in respect of the competency in question.	– "Did the candidate explain there is a perceived conflict of interest for John to act as audit manager in the audit of Metallo?" (A31) This question clearly establishes, from the outset, that the candidate must not only identify the fact that a conflict of interest exists, but explain why. Why is this a conflict of interest? What are the consequences thereof?
Take cognizance of the problem or issue under analysis. One must identify the issues to be resolved in order to clearly establish the direction of the assessment.	– The competency relates to the "potential or actual scope limitation" (A29). – The competency relates to the necessity that the organization advise its audit committee. N.B.: The topic is usually clearly identified in one of the lesser performance levels.
Pay attention to the words used to describe the requirements of the guide. The words "advise", "analyze", "compare", "describe", "discuss", "evaluate", "explain", etc. have their own specific meaning.	– One must "compare" the profitability of each product to the others. In other words, one must state which is the least and the most profitable, as opposed to the standard, if applicable (A24). – "Assess" may mean that one must examine the benefits and disadvantages of two alternatives, such as the decision to develop in-house an electronic data exchange system or outsourcing it.

When you examine each of the competencies in the Competency Grids, pay attention to any crucial or unusual item. Flesh out the key concepts underlying the analysis, such as "comparability" (A24) and "materiality" (A29). Attempt to identify the structure of each solution key, flesh out the components (A18, A19) or underscore the presence of significant items (A21). Note the fact, for instance, that the "Below" level requires a discussion from the union perspective OR the employer perspective, whereas the "Meets" level requires a discussion from the union perspective AND the employer perspective. It may also be that the "Meets" level requires the consideration of a certain number of items, such as the identification of THREE risks of relocating (A22). Do not forget to examine the relation between the case facts (in yellow) and the theoretical concepts (in green). In brief, remain attuned to all that may assist you in understanding how to assess your response.

Analytical objective	Examples of observations
Identify what the "core" of the analysis involves. Identification of problem or issue ↓ Analyze/Evaluation ↓ Recommendation/Advice	– The analysis involves explaining the difference between the GAAP and the CAS in the impact which they have on the work audit and the audit report. (A30) – The analysis involves a discussion of the new factors of inherent risk and the control risk during the fiscal year. – The analysis involves explaining the various means of determining the value of a business.

Analytical objective	Examples of observations
Examine the required scale in order to graduate from one performance level to another. One must identify those items that make a difference in a successful demonstration of competency.	– DESCRIBING the general basic concepts regarding the backup system is at the "Below" level. At the "Meets" level, one must DISCUSS HOW to restore the data: various methods are available. (A21) – IDENTIFYING the strengths and weaknesses of an expansion project is at the "Below" level. At the "Meets" level, one must ANALYZE how it represents a strength or a weakness, in the specific context of the organization. – STATING that the continuous reduction of profitability of the organization has an impact on several aspects of the organization is the "Below" level. At the "Meets" level, one must IDENTIFY how this affects relations with various stakeholders (bank, employees, suppliers). N.B.: The integration of the ideas to the case is usually required at the "Meets" and "Exceeds" levels.
Examine what is required at the "Exceeds" level. Personally, although I know that the "Meets" level is the one to satisfy in order to be successful in the demonstration of a competency, I make sure that I understand what is required at the "Exceeds" level. Knowing where the analysis is heading assists in ensuring that one stays on track.	– In addition to the recommendations, the "Exceeds" level requires a consideration of the information needs of the creditor. – Giving client some tax planning advice is part of the "Exceeds" level. (A18) – Any suggestion to improve the backup system once the current problem has been solved is part of the "Exceeds" level. In other words, that which relates to the short term is at the "Meets" level and that which may take effect in the medium term is at the "Exceeds" level (A21).

Professional qualities and skills

Having good knowledge of the contents of the suggested solution as well as of the contents of the knowledge competencies is an undeniable asset when comes the time to analyze the professional qualities and skills competencies. Succeeding in the core and core-related competencies is, incidentally, regularly a pre-requisite to success in the so-called "professional competencies".

In addition to the competencies in communications, which we find in each case, it is sometimes difficult to anticipate that which will fall under professional qualities and skills. Personally, when I draft my response to a case, I essentially focus on adequately solving the problems or issues. I do not attempt to anticipate the contents of the Competency Grids, in particular those with respect to professional qualities and skills. In order to succeed in a case, it is essential to respond adequately to that which is Required.

One must fully understand what is required at the "Meets" level.

When you analyze professional qualities and skills, draw inspiration first from the advice provided until now. Then, make an effort to clearly highlight that which must be accomplished in order to succeed in each of these competencies. Was I required to discuss the impact on several functions within the business? Was I required to consider the requirements of the stakeholders? (A26) Was I required to discuss the implications from several perspectives? One must ultimately determine specifically why such competency forms part of the Competency Grids, in light of the case parameters. If the two shareholders of an organization have opposite points of view on the environmental issue, you should not be surprised to find the competency "SF: Stakeholder focus" in the Competency Grids.

The Things to Remember

Once the analysis of a case is finished, I suggest that you take several minutes to jot down on a separate piece of paper what are the key items which you have learned from the case. It is quite possible – and I recommend that you do so – that you be required to revisit a case that has already been simulated. Taking several notes on each of them will enable you to find the information you are seeking. Since you have probably jotted down your observations all over your documents, summarizing the essential aspects thereof in the same place will be useful throughout your learning process using the case method.

You will find, on the following page, an illustration of a card you could fill out for the AJX case.

From the outset, you can observe that the notes written on this card are succinct; they may, incidentally, even be further abbreviated. You must pick out what appears to you to be the most important. What is specific to the case? What surprised you? The items of the CONTEXT that deserve to be underscored must be brought to your attention. It is not necessary, for instance, to recall that a public company must follow the IFRS (A14). Do not waste time on items that you are already proficient in. Conducting, for instance, a comparison between the gross margin of the three divisions (A13) may be a natural reflex for you. There is, therefore, no need to write it on the AJX case info-card in order to remind yourself of this step. One must focus on that which you wish to remember in order to better succeed in your next simulations. Your time is precious: one sentence for each comment.

> **COMMENT**
>
> I suggested to you a basic framework in which to state your observations on each simulated case. This card belongs to you and you may certainly add other sections if you so wish. What one wishes to take from a case may vary from one person to the next. The purpose of the info-card on a case is to create a checklist that you might refer to if need be.
>
> Candidates usually fill this form out on the computer in order to easily retrace what they are searching for with key words. Since the case simulation extends over several months, it is often useful to return to the first cases simulated. What you learned from them is still valid and may definitely be reviewed, especially where a professional examination is lurking on the horizon.
>
> Incidentally, I will revisit this aspect in Part 7 of this volume.

Excerpt of an "Info-card on a Case" – AJX Example

Simulation Date: March 15, 2OX3   **Case:** AJX (100 minutes)

Required / Problems or issues:

FA: subs/divisions, reporting period, diff/sim ASPE/IFRS

TX: subs/divisions, purch/lease equip

ET: public health, conflict of interest

...

IMPACT of the particulars of the context on the solution:

International supplier → foreign currency translation; different tax rules; risk

Chemicals products → risk; ethic

Regulated environment → costs; risk

...

Professional qualities and skills:

- IA: INTEGRATE info from Exh; DRAW conclusions from exh; INFORM board impact changes

- OE: ANALYZE various issues + ADVISE on further action

...

Particulars of the suggested solution:

- When five months of financial data are missing, one must raise the potential scope limitation of the audit.

- One must not only mention that the relocation involves such and such a risk, one must also discuss its financial impact.

- Etc.

Particulars of the Competency Grids:

- At the "Meets" level, one must explain the accounting standards or the tax rules. At the "Exceeds" level, one must clearly recommend the appropriate treatment.

- The potential public health issue must be raised. We must see beyond the numbers! Sometimes, complying with the regulations is not enough.

- Etc.

Other observations:

- Although John is not able to conduct the audit of the financial statements due to his lack of independence, he must nevertheless respond to the questions asked by Megan.

- The case presents the information for the three sales divisions located in three different countries. One must highlight the fact that there are tax differences between them, that they do not offer the same profitability and make a recommendation as to the relocation of each of them.

- Etc.

Part 6
Assessing One's Response

Appropriate ideas
Assessment of One's Response
Post-Evaluation of the Performance

"In evaluating the quality of your response, the assessor will look to see if you have grasped the key issues in a case, and were able to problem solve, analyze, integrate, prioritize, and finally, communicate effectively."

Introduction to Issues in Professional Practice, Course description and purpose,
PA1, CGA-Canada, 2012-2013.

PART 6
Assessing One's Response

In my view, assessing one's response is not merely determining what the level of performance achieved was for each of the competencies appearing in the Competency Grids. I quite understand why that is of great interest to you, but it is not the be all and end all. Beyond the results as such, the analysis of your response, viewed in the light of previous results, will enable you to improve your performance for the next case.

Appropriate ideas

I am about to give you a series of suggestions as to how to annotate your own response for analytical purposes. The objective is to be able to potentially flesh out your strengths and your weaknesses. Identifying that which you must improve on for the next simulation is a crucial step when learning according to the case method.

> **COMMENT**
> Some candidates hesitate to write on their own response. I respect that. I suggest that you change colours or simply photocopy your response for analytical purposes. Do not miss out on this opportunity to improve.

First of all, one must flesh out the ideas contained in the response that deserve to be rewarded in the assessment. Not all that is written counts and one frequently notices that certain ideas, even certain paragraphs, are quite simply not considered by the assessor. May I remind you that an idea must be RELEVANT and NEW in order to be considered in the assessment.

I suggest that you highlight your appropriate ideas by underlining them, highlighting them or identifying them using any other sign you like. Case summaries, introductory phrases, discussions of non required items, incomplete ideas – identified by a sign such "+/–", for instance – and, of course, erroneous ideas will not be considered.

> **COMMENT**
> It may happen that you make a mistake in your solution. Of course, the idea does not count. In a taxation discussion, for instance, using the term "net book value" instead of "adjusted cost base", is not appropriate. This does not necessarily invalidate the rest of the discussion, especially if the meaning is adequate, but that does not help your case. One must, therefore, seek, to the extent possible, to use clear and precise terms.
>
> Mathematical errors, generally speaking, are not sanctioned where the concept, in and of itself, is adequate.

It is sometimes difficult to determine if a written idea is sufficiently clear or complete in order to be considered. The question one must ask oneself is whether the recipient of the report will understand what you wanted to say without having to ask you any questions or add any words. The MEANING of the idea presented in the suggested solution or in the Competency Grids must be there. One can use synonyms, but the core of the idea must be there. I suggest that you not consider implicit ideas, for you do not know if the reader of your response will take note of it.

EXAMPLES OF IDEAS CONSIDERED OR NOT CONSIDERED IN THE ASSESSMENT

Idea contained in the suggested solution	Ideas not considered in the assessment	Idea considered in the assessment
"To test the valuation of the scrap inventory, we should try to validate the recorded value by agreeing the value to an outside source."	"To test the valuation of the scrap inventory, we should perform a count of the scrap."	"To test the valuation of the scrap inventory, we should require the help of a specialist."
The major idea related to an audit of the "valuation" assertion. The candidate must set out a procedure to be performed.	This is an adequate procedure in order to test the "existence" of the inventory. It is not a valid procedure to test the "valuation".	The procedure to be performed in order to test the "valuation" assertion is adequate. A "specialist" is an "outside source".
"Presently, the lack of information for the Mexico division can create a potential scope limitation." (A15)	"The lack of information for the Mexico division may affect the audit report."	"The lack of information for the Mexico division is a limitation of the audit that should be mentioned in the report."
The major idea related to the impact of the lack of information. The candidate must demonstrate that he or she understands the manner in which this may affect the audit report.	The impact on the audit report is not expressly mentioned. The candidate perceived this effect ("may") but it is insufficient. HOW? WHAT? SO?	The impact of the lack of information on the audit report is mentioned. Indeed, the text could be a little shorter and it is always preferable to use exact expressions, such as "scope limitation". However, the significant idea is there, and that is what matters.
"The new technology will facilitate the weekly cash forecasting."	"The new technology can be considered in the forecasting process."	"The new technology will facilitate the inflows and outflows forecasting."
The major idea related to the benefit of the new technology. The candidate must demonstrate that he or she knows that this will promote the preparation of the cash forecasting.	The candidate saw the ties between the technology and the forecasting. One must pursue the discussion and state the nature of this relation. What is the benefit?	The terms "inflows and outflows" are acceptable synonyms for the term "cash". It would be preferable to refer to the "weekly" period, but that does not invalidate the essence of the idea.

As you identify the appropriate ideas, I suggest that you write next to them which competency(ies) they relate to. Similarly, you may check off, as you go along, the ideas in the solution key that you have obtained. This will enable you to consider in one single sequence all the ideas relating to the same problem or issue in order to perform a global assessment.

The analysis of one's response is essential to the learning process.

In addition to the foregoing, in order to better analyze your performance, I suggest that you annotate your response in the following manner:

- "REC" ("R") or "CONC" for recommendations or conclusions. Recommendations, for instance, are usually considered at the "Exceeds" level. Assessing the situation, or reaching a conclusion, is sometimes the portal to a core and core-related competency.

  AJX CASE: At the "Substantially below" level, one must recognize the presence of a negative cash balance (A23) or a going concern problem (A30).

- "REP" or Ⓡ for the repetition of the same idea. It is useless to repeat oneself, both in the analysis and the recommendation, for instance. Revisiting the same topic in two different contexts is adequate, but repeating the same idea in other words is pointless.

  AJX CASE: The topic of the "intercompany transactions" must be discussed as an accounting issue (A16) and as a tax issue (A18).

- "+/-" or "INC" for an idea that is more or less clear or complete. These ideas will probably not be considered in the assessment, but it is useful to determine what is missing. An explanation? The meaning of an idea? An impact?

- "W" for weak. This allows you to identify the areas where the theoretical concepts are erroneous or statements are lacking in practical meaning. A review of the theory may be useful!

- "GEN" for a general idea. One may observe that an idea is lacking in concrete definition or practical application. One must see if it is possible to further integrate the ideas to the case. Practise this exercise!

I suggest that, from time to time, you perform the exercise of counting the number of ideas – both relevant and new – which you have written in your response. In so doing, certain candidates realize that they truly do not write much. Some 15 relevant and new ideas for a 100 minute case is insufficient. Filling some 10 pages is good, but one must especially ensure that they contain a sufficient number of ideas for the purposes of the assessment. For instance, dealing with one or two changes to be made to the financial statements in accordance with IFRS will be insufficient at the "Meets" level, even if the ideas put forth are accurate and are presented with a substantiated recommendation (A27).

Where your response is analyzed and commented in the manner described above, it is then easier to identify what is wrong with the manner in which you resolve cases. One must ask oneself questions and seek a solution to any weakness identified. The objective is to constantly improve your performance as well as the efficiency of your writing. You may, for instance, cross out everything you consider to be useless in your response. You may also decide to redraft a section that was especially poor.

© CGA = COMPETENCY

Examples of questions you should ask yourself

Questions to ask oneself	Comments	Solutions
Where are the relevant and new ideas located?	It is not infrequent that a candidate will summarize the case prior to beginning the resolution thereof. Or, he or she will set out an elaborate theoretical summary before revisiting the key concepts in order to apply them to the case.	– Summarize in your head or very succinctly on a worksheet where this is essential. – Only focus on the theoretical concepts that are required for the resolution of a problem or issue.
Are there aspects of the suggested solution or of the Competency Grids which have been neglected?	A candidate may have some difficulty in identifying so-called "non-directed" questions. Otherwise, he or she may present the analysis of the problems or issues in the order in which they appear in the case or, even worse, he or she may concentrate on secondary issues.	– Pay attention to any hint in the case which is meant to open up the discussion of a problem or issue, at least *ex post facto*. – Take the time to assess the significance of the topics in order to ensure that you deal with all the primary problems or issues (important) and a part of the others
Does the analysis of the problems or issues have sufficient depth?	A candidate might proceed too quickly to the goal without assessing the various alternatives or otherwise not sufficiently explain his or her ideas. He or she may also neglect to write the easiest ideas, on the basis that they are obvious!	– Take the time to develop the analysis when faced with an important problem or issue. – Show the steps of the logical reasoning followed prior to making any recommendations or conclusions.

Assessment of One's Response

In respect of each of the competencies set out in the Competency Grids, you must attribute a "score". Personally, I build a simplified grid for each of the cases which I simulate. The purpose is to be able to quickly refer to all the results achieved, mainly the 22 competencies appearing in the AJX case for instance, on a single page if possible. You are free to add any other information. The items making up the "ANALYSE/EVALUATION" section or that which is required at the "Meets" level, for instance, could certainly be useful.

Slowly but surely, one gets closer to the "Meets" level.

RESULTS ACHIEVED FOR THE AJX CASE

Competency	Problem or issue	0	1	2	3	4
FA	Differences between subsidiaries and sales division				X	
FA	Different reporting period end dates			X		
TX	Differences between subsidiaries and sales division				X	
Etc.	...					

Generally speaking, the results of all the candidates who have seen or discussed a problem or issue are essentially allocated between the "Below" level and the "Meets" level. Therefore, it is in the area between these two levels of performance that a successful demonstration of competency plays out, and maybe even the success of the case. When you assess your response, you must, therefore, make sure that you have fully understood all that is required at the "Meets" level. This is the "key" level.

COMMENT

Correcting one's own response is not an easy exercise. It requires objectivity and detachment. One must only reward those appropriate ideas which are part of your response, BLACK ON WHITE. One must not tell oneself "I know this theory" or "I wanted to state this", or again: "I would surely have written this under exam conditions!". If it is not written, and even rather clearly, it will not be considered in the assessment. The assessor of your examination possesses no other information besides what you have written.

I also urge you to correct all the cases that you have simulated. Sometimes, because they know in advance that they did not do very well, certain candidates do not conduct this exercise. However, I know from experience that it is very profitable to analyze one's answers in order to do better the next time around.

Here are examples of candidates followed by a commented assessment of their performance.

AJX CASE: EXAMPLE OF RESPONSE #1 – ETHICS AND TRUST (A20)

Metallo's management is considering producing the Standard product in Mexico where no bans on this chemicals exist. Also, Metallo management feels that the Industrial product would be better manufactured in Mexico due to more business-friendly regulations.

I don't like that! These are not acceptable manners of functioning and it may be harmful to the organization.

ASSESSMENT: Performance level 2 "Below"

The issue is adequately identified and justified using the case facts. It is obvious that the candidate recognized Metallo's unethical business practices. The fact that the word "ethics" is absent from the response is not particularly troublesome, since the concept has been presented in other words. Seeing that this may be harmful to the organization is good, but one must state why. The analysis is therefore INCOMPLETE AS TO THE IMPACT of the policies considered and this is the "core" of the analysis of this competency. As for the writing style as such, the first paragraph is a summary of the case which is too long. "I don't like that" is not business language.

AJX CASE: EXAMPLE OF RESPONSE #2 – ETHICS AND TRUST (A20)

> The business practices of Metallo are clearly unethical.
>
> This can have a negative impact on the clients.
>
> I recommend to not move the production to Mexico for this reason.

> **ASSESSMENT: Performance level 2 "Below"**

This short response is incomplete. The issue is clearly identified. The impact has been considered, but NOT SUFFICIENTLY EXPLAINED. The recommendation is adequate and will potentially be considered at the "Exceeds" level. The presence of a recommendation does not, however, discharge the candidate from presenting a sufficiently complete analysis of the impacts of the unethical business practices. Too often, candidates correctly identify a problem or issue, and then jump directly (or nearly directly) to the recommendation without explaining the steps they have followed. Without the ANALYZE/EVALUATION section, no "Meets" level!

At the "Meets" level, a certain depth of analysis is required. Indeed, one does not expect that all the ideas – or their equivalent – as listed in the solution key will be referred to by the candidate, but a certain number of them must be. In the example above, there were only three relevant and new ideas, written in three sentences, including only one in the "ANALYZE" section. This is not sufficient.

The two previous examples share a common thread: All the candidate wrote is accurate. It lacks relevance or depth, but it is not erroneous. When you do not achieve the "Meets" level – and this will happen to you quite often –, do not become discouraged, since you are perhaps not lacking very much in order to achieve it.

AJX CASE: EXAMPLE OF RESPONSE #3 – ETHICS AND TRUST (A20)

> The reasons why Metallo is moving production to Mexico are not valid. These are unethical business practices.
>
> Moving production can have strong and unpredictable negative impacts. Clients and governments can be upset by the fact that Metallo does not want to follow the laws. Public in general is very sensitive when its health is concerned, so the reputation of Metallo can suffer as a result. On a long-term horizon, clients can be lost.

> **ASSESSMENT: Performance level 3 "Meets"**

The issue is clearly identified. The analysis part is well done and contains, if you want to count it, five relevant and new ideas. Based on case facts, this candidate is discussing the impact of the business practices of Metallo. The words are not exactly the same as the suggested solution or the Competency Grids, since the word "law" is used instead of "regulation". However, the sense is clearly there.

To get the level "Exceeds", this candidate should end his analysis with, I would say, one strong recommendation.

N.B.: Generally speaking, the "Exceeds" level is awarded where one recommendation "supported by the analysis" is made. One must understand that it is not only sufficient to justify the recommendation, it must be supported by the analysis. In other words, the "Meets" level must be awarded prior to accessing the "Exceeds" level. Personally, I make the effort of suggesting more than one recommendation on important topics.

Finally, note the efficiency of the drafting. The sentences are short; one idea is developed per sentence. The ideas are clear and precise. The arguments are responsible; the candidate assumes the position he or she is advancing. The impact is mentioned in social and financial terms.

Allow me to revisit an important point, namely what one must do at the "Meets" level, since this is the level that makes the difference. Remember this: you must provide added value to your response. A candidate that only IDENTIFIES or STATES a problem or issue, LISTS case facts, or DISCUSSES or DESCRIBES basic concepts cannot hope to obtain anything more than the "Below" level. Take a step back and examine your response. What have you done more? And is it sufficiently in-depth? Make sure that you always understand what the "value-added" component that is required at the "Meets" level is.

COMMENT

If possible, I suggest that you exchange your response for that of a colleague. The assessment by this colleague will very likely be more objective than yours. He or she, for instance, may identify weaknesses which did not think of. This is also a good means of assessing the quality of your writing. Also, by reading the response of another person, this enables you to take cognizance of the various manners of drafting. Observing the analytical process of a candidate who achieved a better result than yours is a profitable exercise.

When you submit your response to another assessor, colleague or moderator, conduct your own assessment nevertheless. You could subsequently compare the two results in order to identify those areas where you experience some difficulty assessing your own performance.

In order to complement my explanations as to the manner of assessing your response, here are a few additional TIPS to consider.

One must:

- *Read the Baseline Question.* The significant items to be considered in the assessment of the competency are set out in this short question. This assists in determining what is essential to success. From the outset, you could very well respond by YES or NO. You will then know if you satisfied the "Meets" level.

- *Take into Account the Level of Performance You are Aiming For.* You already know that the "Meets" level makes the difference. I suggest, therefore, that you be a little more demanding in awarding this level. One can be slightly more generous when awarding the "Below" level, but not where a successful demonstration of a competency is at play. The "Exceeds" level, which is not very often awarded, usually requires the presence of concrete, precise, recommendations that are integrated to the particulars of the case.

- *Consider the Presence of "Other" Valid Points.* The Competency Grids usually allow for a consideration of other ideas than those which they contain. For instance, in example #3 presented above, it is, therefore, possible for you to consider in the assessment a RELEVANT AND NEW idea, even if you do not find it as such in the official solution of the case. Obviously, this does not mean that any idea will be accepted. Remember that the suggested solution, as well as the Competency Grids, contain the most important ideas with respect to a problem or issue.

One must not:

- *Believe that the Successful Demonstration of a Competency Positively Influences the Assessment of the Others*, and *vice versa*. In the AJX case, for instance, a candidate may very well pass the various competencies for financial accounting and experience difficulty in achieving the "Below" level in Taxation. Usually, each competency is assessed independently from the others and the assessor starts from scratch each time.

  However, I remind you that the professional quality and skill competencies generally take into account part or all of the response to the case.

- *Compensate a Missing Item by Another.* Discussing a secondary issue, for instance, cannot compensate for the absence of primary issues. Hence, submitting good recommendations does not make up for the lack of depth of analysis required at the "Meets" level. And a theoretical summary, even if it is very well done, cannot compensate for a need for integration to the case.

- *Consider Ideas Without any Concern for their Quality or Significance.* One must constantly bear in mind that only relevant and new ideas count. Indeed, one must write a certain number of them, but they must essentially bear on that which is IMPORTANT. Writing a great wealth of ideas if not always a guarantee of success. For instance, one must flesh out the "significant" risk factors for the next audit. Spending time on general factors or rather insignificant factors will not suffice.

Post-Evaluation of the Performance

When you have just assessed your response to a case, I suggest that you draw up a list of your strengths and weaknesses. Start with the strengths TO BE KEPT. Too often, one forgets them and it is very motivating to identify what we did right. As for weaknesses, I will confess that they are quite abundant, in particular during the first case simulations. When you have just concluded the analysis of a case, I suggest that you identify the three most significant weaknesses TO WORK ON. Ask yourself which are those which most stood in the way of your success. Since it is impossible to progress on all fronts at the same time, one should establish priorities. For instance, knowing how to flesh out non-directed problems or issues is much more important than seeking to cut down on the length of one's sentences. At some point in time, one will have to focus on this latter issue, but a little bit later.

COMMENT

It appears to me to be important to set concrete learning objectives to achieve during the drafting of the next case. Too often, candidates tell themselves: "I will do better next time!".

Fine, but with respect to what and how? Improving one's performance with respect to the resolution of cases is a process that extends over several months. One step at a time is the only way to achieve that goal.

In order not to lose sight of the goals to be achieved, certain candidates display them prominently on their work desk. Others create a giant table setting out a series of objectives, as well as their progress over time.

Here is an example.

EXCERPT OF THE TABLE "FOLLOW-UP OF MY LEARNING OBJECTIVES"

Learning objectives	AJX case March 15, 20X3	Case ABC	Case XYZ
Fleshing out the non-directed problems or issues	Incomplete Ethic issue not seen (A20)		
Knowing what to do with the financial data of the case	Very good Gross margin compared (A24)		
Consider the impact of the problems or issues identified	Not always Did not see the impact on the financial position (A22) Did not see the impact on audit report (A30)		
Etc.	...		

It appears to me to be also essential to acquire the means in order to determine what competencies are the ones with which you experienced the most difficulty. It is not always obvious to identify this information, on the one hand, because cases are very different from each other and, on the other hand, because the consequences of the same type, such as "Financial Accounting", are not always presented one after the other (A16, A17, A27). In addition, since one can state that a case has been successful without the "Meets" level having been satisfied in respect of each of the competencies, it is easy to forget to consider the performance of the competencies taken individually or by sub groups. One must afford oneself the possibility of observing which competencies need work.

Some candidates write all their results in a file, such as an Excel document. Based on the table presented previously for each of the simulated cases (page 56), they create a separate tab for each type of competency. This enables them to observe, for instance, that the level of performance achieved for the "Information technology" competency is constantly at the "Substantially below" level or "Below" level. This is then a sign which should not be neglected.

It is especially revealing to examine one's performance in this manner when dealing with professional qualities and skills competencies. A candidate who, for instance, is unable to demonstrate that he or she can "integrate and analyze data for patterns, relationships, and trends" (Professional scepticism) (A26), simulation after simulation, must absolutely do something.

COMMENT

I strongly urge you to persevere. Case analysis is a learning process which is not always easy. Success in a case today does not mean that the one you are faced with tomorrow will also be successful (and *vice versa*). Over a certain time period, one usually observes an improvement, but in the day-to-day study, it is not always so simple.

One can always improve one's performance in case resolution, even the day after passing an official examination. Keep focussing on your learning objectives, analyze your cases meticulously and have confidence in your abilities.

Part 7
Studying Simulated Cases

Inter-Cases Comparison
Theoretical Concepts
Preparation of an Examination

"Competency development continues throughout a CGA's career."

CGA Competency framework, CGA-Canada, 2010, p. 8.

PART 7
Studying Simulated Cases

As your learning according to the case method progresses, it becomes possible to cast a more comprehensive view of simulated cases. We know that each case is unique, owing to the specific parameters that characterize it. There are, therefore, several differences from one case to the next, which require flexibility in terms of adaptation and the exercise of professional judgment. There are also similarities. Discovering the similarities and understanding the differences between prior cases will help you to better resolve cases in the future.

Inter-Cases Comparison

Taking a step back and conducting comparisons between simulated cases enables you to better understand the structure of the suggested solution and the manner in which the Competency Grids are built. One can then highlight the manners of proceeding which may accelerate the drafting of your next case.

> **COMMENT**
>
> In this Part, the analytical approach I suggest is different from that which is usually taught. Common usage suggests that one should analyze cases one at a time. That is the objective of Part 6 where, for instance, each of the competencies in the Competency Grids is studied.
>
> In Part 7, the cases are decompartmentalized in order to conduct a cross-sectional analysis of their components, with a view, among others, to comparing the roles, the response structures and the assessment of competencies.

The Role

We know that relevant ideas to be developed in the resolution of a case must take into account parameters that are specific to it: the Required elements, the role and the context. The role to be played influences the angle according to which the facts of the case are examined. There is indeed quite a difference between acting as an accountant in-house (PA2) or acting as an external accountant (PA1, AP1).

NOTEWORTHY DIFFERENCES IN THE ROLE TO BE PLAYED

Problem or issue	Role
The Required elements request that you discuss audit procedures to be performed.	– The external auditor will determine the procedures to be performed in light of the risk areas he or she will have established previously. Referring to assertions is often useful. N.B.: Drafting a procedure can take the following form: "To ensure/test that…, we need to…". – The role of the internal auditor is much broader since the latter must, among others, assess the adequacy and effectiveness of internal control system, as well as the compliance with corporate policies. This goes beyond the framework of the audit assertions.

Problem or issue	Role
The Required elements request that you discuss the potential impact of the new bonus program.	– The external auditor will consider the increase in the inherent risk because the new bonus program is based on the gross margin. – The external consultant will consider the potential impact from several angles. The motivation of the employees and the adequacy of the steps taken in light of the objectives sought to be achieved may be examined.
The Required elements request that you establish the value of the organization in the context of an impending sale.	– The external consultant must know if he or she is working with the vendor or the purchaser. Of course, he or she may not represent both parties at the same time. An accountant will favour the position of his or her client, while remaining honest. – For instance, following the establishment of a price range [$2,500,000- $2,700,000], an accountant would suggest to his or her vendor client that the latter ask, from the outset, the highest amount, namely $2,700,000. The accountant representing the purchaser, on the other hand, will suggest making a preliminary offer at $2,500,000. There will, thereafter, be negotiation between both parties.

The Response Structures

As discussed in Part 3 (page 22), the fundamental drafting structure is the following:

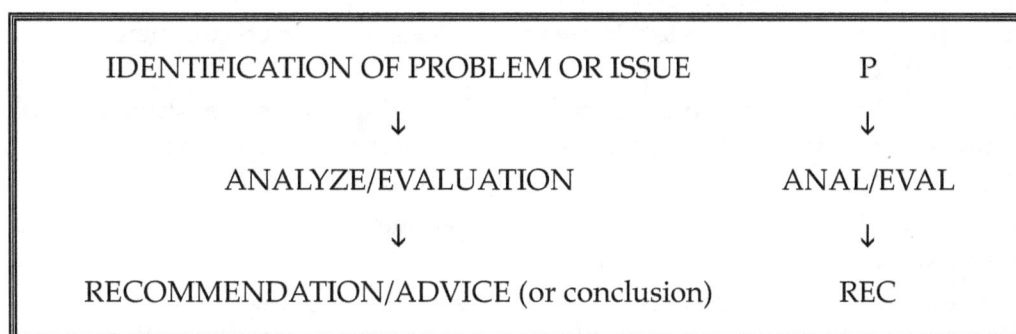

```
IDENTIFICATION OF PROBLEM OR ISSUE        P
                ↓                          ↓
        ANALYZE/EVALUATION            ANAL/EVAL
                ↓                          ↓
RECOMMENDATION/ADVICE (or conclusion)      REC
```

It appears to me to be useful to highlight the components of the Analyze /Evaluation part, specifically that which is required at the "Meets" performance level. The examination of the suggested solutions enables you to flesh out the response structures which are repetitive, for a Required element, a role or a context. In other words, the idea is to highlight the steps of the resolution of a given problem or issue. The objective of this exercise is to assist you in determining the steps to take under certain circumstances in a quicker fashion.

INFO-CARD – RESPONSE STRUCTURE

Where there are alternatives to be considered with a view to making a decision, one must discuss the benefits and disadvantages of each of them.

- E.g.: sell or process, make or buy, buy or lease, etc.
- Since it is a "LIST OF", the benefits and disadvantages may be expressed in a more abbreviated fashion. Their meaning, however, must be obvious. Writing "quality of the products" is insufficient in the list of the benefits to manufacturing in-house. One should instead say something such as "better quality control of the products".

  N.B.: One must examine both sides: "pros-cons"and "risks-opportunities".
- The analysis takes into account the facts of the case and knowledge in general.
- One must conclude the analysis by recommending the alternative which seems to be the most appropriate under the circumstances. It must be supported by the analysis.
- Where calculations are necessary, they must be interpreted. They accompany the qualitative analysis but do not replace it.
- Etc.

COMMENT

It appears to me to be necessary to bring together the information gathered in the inter-cases comparison in order to be able to refer to it quickly. Personally, I create what I refer to as "info-cards" which succinctly summarize the ideas fleshed out during the analysis. The info-cards are created for your personal benefit, and, therefore, you must ensure that they meet your needs.

INFO-CARD – RESPONSE STRUCTURE

Where there are internal control weaknesses to discuss, one must mention the impacts or consequences of these weaknesses, and then recommend improvements.

- A brief recap of the objectives sought to be achieved by establishing control procedures, or a brief discussion of the importance of correcting any weaknesses detected, forms a regular part of the discussion.
- When such is not clearly set out in the case, one must specify why there is a weakness, in light of the case facts.
- The discussion with respect to each of the weaknesses must not be very long, since there are usually several that have been detected. In other words, since we are usually aiming for BREADTH over DEPTH, a certain number of weaknesses must be discussed.
- The recommended improvements must be concrete and precise so that a non-management employee will know exactly WHAT DO TO. It may be appropriate to state WHO will act and WHEN he or she will do so. If possible, refer directly to the employees and documents of the organization.

N.B.: An analysis of the business risks, such as the analysis of the "risks associated with relocating the manufacturing" (A22) follows nearly the same response structure.

> The inter-cases comparison
> highlights the similarities between cases.
> However, no one can predict with certainty
> what will make up the next case.

COMMENT

As you progress through simulations, the fact that you prepared an "info-card" on a case is very useful when you wish to analyze the various manners in which the same topic, problem or issue is analyzed. (Part 5, page 50)

Assessment of the Competencies

I know from experience that it is very revealing to compare the solution keys of competencies of the same type. What must one do in order to achieve the "Meets" performance level of an "Ethics and trust" competency or a "Finance" competency? What I suggest is that you concentrate on the "Analyze/Evaluation" part, per type of competency.

INFO-CARD – "ETHICS AND TRUST" COMPETENCY

- The identification of the ethical issue is usually necessary at the "Below" level, and sometimes at the "Substantially below" level.
- At the "Meets" level, one must either explain why it is an ethical issue or explain what the consequences thereof are.
- One must regularly refer to the *Code of Ethical Principles and Rules of Conduct* (CEPROC). (A31)
- Do not lose sight of the concept of "protect the public interest". (A20)
- Etc.

COMMENT

When comparing solutions keys for the same type of competency, certain candidates can physically group them together. Some simply "cut and paste" all the solution keys in a single file. Others print them up, cut them out, and paste them on a large cardboard. Choose the method which works best for you in order to observe and analyze the similarities and differences between the various competencies in the program. And, especially, insist on the competencies that cause you the greatest difficulty.

Info-card – "Financial Accounting" Competency

When dealing with financial accounting issues, one must correctly explain the accounting standards. For a newly-certified CGA, this is a must.

- Knowing basic accounting concepts is usually required at the "Below" level, and even sometimes at the "Substantially below" level.
- There is really no margin for error in financial accounting. One must know the theoretical concepts! (A16, A19)
- Simply setting out the accounting standards is insufficient; one must explain them, and sometimes describe the impact on the financial statements.
- A link integrated to the users of the financial statements is a value-added item to the discussion. (A17)
- The analysis concludes by clear and precise recommendations as to the accounting treatment to adopt.
- Etc.

N.B.: Any comments one may make regarding tax issues are similar. One must know the tax rules well, state them, and then explain them, if need be.

The exercise of comparing the various solution keys of a same type of competencies is especially useful with respect to professional qualities and skills. Examining all at once what is involved in the "Integrative approach", the "Stakeholder focus" or the "Professional scepticism", for instance, allows one to take stock of the various situations requiring such a professional competency. We know that there are no two identical cases, but knowing what may make up such and such a competency is certainly an asset. In the AJX case, for instance, integrating the information taken from the exhibits in the analysis of the problems or issues is assessed by the "Integrative approach" competency (A25). This is professional skill to remember for future cases.

When I conduct my inter-cases comparison, I frequently identify cause-to-effect relationships that I wish to remember. I summarize them in short sentences, that may be expressed as follows: "When there is/are…, you should consider…". For instance,

Info-card – Relationships

When there is/are…,	You should consider…
a planned acquisition of another business,	a due diligence investigation.
a specialized industry,	to consult a specialist.
cash flow problems,	the going concern issue. (A28)
an audit materiality discussion,	the needs of users.
high fixed costs,	the break-even point.
a potential fraud,	a forensic audit.
a limited production capacity,	the opportunity costs.

Whenever possible, schedule a group meeting with your colleagues and take the opportunity to exchange impressions. The observations you have acquired as a result of your inter-cases comparison may be improved in this fashion. For instance, taking each of the professional qualities and skills competencies and discussing their components is very useful, if not reassuring. Similarly, sharing your knowledge on the manner of resolving various problems or issues may help to make the resolution of your cases more efficient.

Theoretical Concepts

Knowing how to resolve a case is essential to success. In fact, that is the purpose of this volume. One must, nevertheless, remember that any response technique, no matter how sophisticated, cannot make up for a lack of knowledge. As indicated above, knowing the basic theoretical concepts in financial accounting barely allows you to achieve the "Substantially below" performance level, and sometimes the "Below" level. If you do not know the theoretical concepts, your ability to present your ideas efficiently, for instance, will not be very helpful. One must also know WHEN to use and HOW to incorporate the theoretical concepts in the case.

> **One must discover means
> in order to remember the key theoretical concepts.**

I suggest that you prepare subject info-cards, if need be, when the topic is revisited regularly in cases, where it is current, where you have difficulty in assimilating it or where it is complex, this is a good idea. Each candidate has specific needs and the info-cards are, therefore, different from one person to the next. Building these cards is an active study method which facilitates the retention of ideas and concepts. I conceive of two parts to this card, namely the theoretical part and the practical part, which are presented all together. Personally, I first flesh out the key components of a topic, using several precise words, or even a short sentence. It may be a theoretical concept or a feature inherent to the topic in question. Thereafter, I add to these items concrete examples, most of the time drawn from simulated cases.

The items highlighted on an info-card are used as a guide and are, to a certain extent, a reference "checklist" that can be used in the resolution of a case. This does not mean that all that appears on a "Performance measures" card, for instance, will appear in all cases that broach this topic. One regularly finds some of these items, NOT ALL OF THEM EACH TIME. When you are drafting, and you are required to discuss performance measures, the "checklist" above will avoid you running out of ideas.

INFO-CARD – PERFORMANCE MEASURES

- alignment with corporate strategy and objectives

  E.g.: Measure = # of kilos of abnormal spoilage, since one of the objectives is the minimization of costs.

- financial AND non-financial measures

  E.g.: Measure = delivery lead time, since it is a key success factor

- Scorecard: financial, customer, internal process, learning and growth

  E.g.: Customer perspective: monthly return on sales

  E.g.: Learning and growth perspective: turnover of mechanics

- based on controllable elements (evaluation or compensation purposes)

- objective of the measure ≠ measure by itself

  E.g.: Maximize profitability is an objective, not a measure. Margin (%) is.

- clear, short and concrete measures! Measures must be measurable!

  E.g.: Measure = number of claims to the customer services is more concrete than simply saying "Measure = client satisfaction".

- benchmark! with previous years or with the industry

- financial system must be able to capture data

- link with mission when not-profit organization

  E.g.: Measure = number of families having taken advantage of the assistance provided

- Etc.

It is useful, if not instructive, to perform, from time to time, the exercise of examining at the same time a problem or issue that arose in more than one case. This allows you both to review the theoretical concepts as well as to examine the manner in which they are analyzed, within the case parameters.

COMMENT

Too often, I meet candidates who prepare many summaries and cards, but who never re-read them. They are always waiting for the right time, which never comes, or occurs too close to an official examination. I suggest that you take, say 15 minutes per day, three times a week, to read your cards, part by part. Once everything has been read, you simply start over, since, in the meantime, you will have improved on your info-cards. It is certainly not useful to learn by heart the list of items which may appear in a discussion on "hedging activities", for instance. Believe me when I say that regularly re-reading one's cards is a good method for remembering them, with a view to an efficient use during the examination.

When you are asked to summarize a topic, I suggest that you draw diagrams (A30) or create tables. Whenever possible, do not hesitate. A table is much better at highlighting the similarities, the differences, as well as the cause-to-effect relationships. Writing the text in some form of a list also enables you to better synthesize and visualize the information.

Risk assessment
↓
Materiality
↓
Audit approach
↓
Specific risks and procedures

Here are illustrations of tables you could prepare:

International Financial Reporting Standards (IFRS)	Accounting Standards for Private Enterprises (ASPE)
...	...

Assertion	Examples of audit procedures
...	...

Benefits of incorporation	Disadvantages of incorporation
...	...

Tax rules – partnership	Tax rules – private company	Tax rules – public company
...	...	...

You could create a card, a table or draw a diagram as soon as a weakness is discovered. If a candidate experiences difficulty with the topic of "Foreign currency translation", for instance, he or she must find ways to fix the problem. Going over texts on the topic in order to highlight the key elements, then analyzing, with some detachment, all the cases dealing with the topic (A11) is a good learning method.

The following is a non-exhaustive list of topics which could be analyzed in this matter, if need be.

- Examples of inherent risk factors / control risk factors
- Examples of internal controls with respect to the segregation of duties, authorization, safeguards, etc.
- Budgeting process
- Available approaches to move from an existing information system to a new one (parallel, direct cutover, phased installation, pilot conversion, etc.) (pros & cons)
- Methods to backup data (removable, fixed, remote, etc.) (A21)
- Particulars of non-profit organizations
- Differences between a Review and an Audit

Preparation of an Examination

By way of conclusion to this volume, I wish to provide you with a few TIPS when you are about to write a professional CGA examination. I suggest that you:

☺ *Stop simulating cases in the days before the examination.* Although I am not able to explain the phenomenon entirely, I know from experience that simulating cases up to the day before an examination is not a good idea. Whether due to nervousness or fatigue, candidates usually do not do very well on these latter cases, and become discouraged, which is, one must say, rather stressful!

- *Read and re-read your cards, notes and observations.* There are very precious sources of information and, the day before an examination, they are the last documents you will read.

- *Review the topics or situations where you know you have weaknesses.* Hence, making the time to take one last look at those cases – or parts of cases – which you did the most poorly on is a useful exercise. Do not fall into the trap of reviewing only those topics which you like or only those with which you have no difficulty.

When writing your examination, I would like to remind you of three fundamentals that you should never lose sight of

- **Stay within the bounds of the time allotted to each of the cases.** Since the time you go over the time allotted to a case penalizes you for the following case, you must be disciplined in this respect. If the resolution of the multiple choice questions leaves you with a few extra minutes, spread them out between the shorter cases.

> **COMMENT**
>
> I know from experience that a 4 hour examination is very demanding, especially if it is scheduled in the evening. Therefore, it is a good idea to prepare for it in order to not find oneself at a loss when the time comes to writing it. There is no doubt that simulating cases on a regular basis, within the allotted time frame, is a very good starting point. I strongly suggest that you simulate during four consecutive hours the CGA practice exams by replicating as closely as possible the conditions of the real examination. Also, studying in blocks of four hours – and minimizing as much as possible any interruptions – is also a good preparation method.

- *Aim to resolve all the primary problems or issues (important) and part of the others.* Be efficient in your writing. Write as many RELEVANT and NEW ideas as possible, in a clear and succinct manner. Integrate your ideas to the case. Make sure that you present a sufficient analysis before proceeding to recommendations. In other words, search for that which will make up the "added value" in the analyze/evaluation segment of the problems or issues.

  Advise, Analyze, Compare, Describe, Discuss, Evaluate, Explain, etc.

- *Trust in your ideas and in your judgment.* In the heat of the action, we are not always very good judges. The examination appears to you to be difficult? That is normal... and the same goes for all the candidates. You are caught off guard when faced with a case? Go through the usual steps, that will reassure you. This is certainly not the right time to "test" new methods!

  When you are not quite sure where to start, start with one of the important problems or issues with which you are the most comfortable. The rest will follow.

I wish you all great success and

Thank you for appreciating my work.

EXHIBIT A

Ajax Metals

(100 minutes)

Issues in Professional Practice Exam [PA1] Practice Exam
published by the Certified General Accountants Association of Canada,
© CGA-Canada, (2012). Reproduced with permission.

This Exhibit, which illustrates how to read a comprehensive case and to analyze the
suggested solution and the Competency Grids, takes its inspiration from the volume
Teachings Tips for Accounting Cases, published by AB + Publications in 2012.

Comprehensive Case Analysis
Ajax Metals (100 minutes) *a*

IFRS

Ajax Metals (AJX) is a <mark>public</mark> company whose shares trade on the Toronto Stock Exchange; a portion of its organizational structure is provided in Exhibit 4-1. AJX is an <mark>international supplier of chemicals</mark> *RISK* for use in pesticides, fertilizer, and industrial applications, with a head office in Regina, Saskatchewan. Metallo is a wholly owned subsidiary of AJX. Metallo's head office is located in Toronto, Ontario. Metallo has three manufacturing and sales divisions: Canada (Ontario), U.S. (California), and Mexico. Each division <mark>only sells</mark> the products <mark>in its own country</mark>. Metallo also conducts transactions with AJX Financial Services Inc. (AJXFSI), a company situated in a country that levies <mark>no income taxes</mark>. AJX owns several other subsidiaries, but Metallo does not have any transactions with them. AJX's management and board of directors <mark>monitor the decisions and activities</mark> of all of its subsidiaries.

BUS/FA

EXHIBIT 4-1 _____

AJX Inc.
Partial Management Organizational Structure

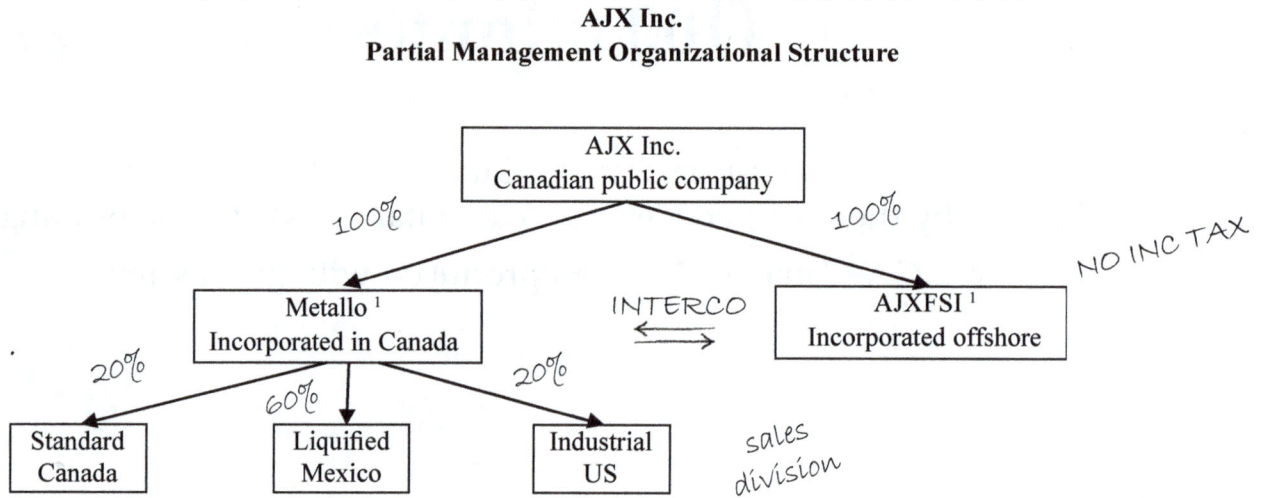

¹ These subsidiaries are 100% owned by AJX Inc. *b*

_____

a For the purposes of presentation of this volume, and to allow me to add comments, the AJX case is presented on a greater number of pages than the original case published by CGA-Canada. When reading, the relevant case facts were highlighted in yellow, whereas everything that concerned the requirements was highlighted in green. Comments that a candidate could write down on the case itself were written in the font used here.

N.B.: Since annotations are used by the candidate only, words are abbreviated. Thus, one will find "IFRS", "BUS" (business), "FA" (financial accounting), "interco" (intercompany), "inc" (income), "TAX" (taxation), "R" (risk), "CA" (Canada), "LT" (long term), "FMV" (fair market value), "MX" (Mexico), "equip" (equipment), "OBJ" (objective), "IMP" (important), "rel part" (related parties), "ACCT" (accounting), "subs" (subsidiaries), "M" (months), etc.

b Personally, I write the essence of the information read on the diagram supplied. This allows me to better understand the situation since the information is centralized at the same place.

Product and sales information *R*

Metallo manufactures three types of chemicals through each of the above divisions: *a*

[margin: relocation]

1. Standard: for direct application as a pesticide for cosmetic purposes to end-user consumers on lawns, golf courses, and parks

2. Liquified: for bulk blending in pesticides and herbicides for agricultural purposes

3. Industrial: for use as a raw material in plastic products to make them flexible and for use in some consumer products such as perfumes, soaps, and lotions

Metallo's manufacturing divisions have been operating near capacity for several years. In 2010, approximate sales for each of the products were 20% in Ontario, 60% in California, and 20% in Mexico. Due to the banning of pesticides for cosmetic purposes in Ontario, sales are expected to decrease significantly in that division. *R*

[margin: regulations]
[margin: ↓ sales CA]

Because of AJX's overall strategy in managing the supply of chemicals on the markets, the amount of finished goods held by Metallo's divisions in inventory is minimal. Metallo's senior management determines the selling prices for all markets and informs the divisions' managers of the pricing structure. Prices are based on variable costs, shipping, and a standard mark-up that covers fixed costs and provides a steady profit level.

[margin: pricing policy]

Metallo's current operating loan was made at a Canadian bank's Regina branch. Long-term financing required for plant and equipment has been provided by AJXFSI. AJXFSI also provides data processing and accounting services for Metallo. The financing and administration expenses paid to AJXFSI are calculated at 30% of revenue. This payment covers both the financing (interest) and the administrative services. !?!

[margin: a. TAX interco]
*[margin: interco:
- LT financing
- current activities]*

Metallo's financial statements are provided in Exhibit 4-2.

Current issues *b*

Megan, a CGA, has been Metallo's external accountant for several years. The internal accounting department records all transactions, but Megan prepares the year-end financial statements and the tax returns for Metallo. She also provides general business advice. *c* At year end, she provides schedules and working papers to AJX's auditors for their report on the consolidated statements. It is early December 2010, and AJX's board of directors has asked Megan to assist with the following two issues:

[margin: no conflict]

---

a In the first paragraph of the case, we learn that "Each division only sells the products in its own country." By reading further, we learn that each division, located in three different countries, bears the name of the single product it manufactures.

b This title "Current Issues" must attract your attention. Formerly, the information supplied was essentially descriptive. It allows you to better understand the organization and operations so as to make your response more relevant. Later on, the information supplied is used to identify each of the problems or issues to be resolved, in light of the case parameters. The problems or issues required are written in the left-hand margin in order to be able to return to the information in quicker fashion during the drafting of the response.

c One must identify the particulars of the context of the organization throughout the reading process: the size of the organization, the industry sector, the key success factors, the strengths, the weaknesses, opportunities and threats, the objectives, needs, preferences, bias and responsibilities of stakeholders, constraints, the business policies, the features of managerial behaviour, etc. Any of these items of information could be useful to explain a problem, analyze an issue or justify a recommendation.

relocation

CA: Standard (cosmetic) ⟶ MX: Standard
MX: Liquified (agricultural) ⟶ CA: Liquified

a. 1. *Divisional structure* [a]

R: agric. market — ethic — a. TAX purchase OR lease

Metallo is considering changing the products manufactured at each of the locations. Since pesticides for cosmetic purposes are now prohibited for sale in Ontario, Metallo's management is considering producing the Standard product in Mexico where the market is readily available and no bans on these chemicals exist. The Liquified product would be moved to Ontario where it is felt that the chemicals used in agriculture may attract purchases from rural consumers. These sales may become possible by allowing agricultural producers to indirectly sell these products. An informal survey conducted with agricultural producers in Ontario indicated they are willing to acquire excess amounts of the Liquified product in order to supply rural purchasers. [b] Metallo would need to invest in new equipment for the Ontario location in order to re-package the product because the recently purchased equipment has proven to be problematic for changing package sizes. This packaging equipment can be purchased new for $3 million, or leased for low monthly payments. Metallo management would like to maximize deductions associated with the equipment to lower the taxable income.

R — regulations — lot of uncertainties! — equip — OBJ

US: Industrial (plastic) ⟶ MX

ethic — R: inflation — FA — FA

Recently, the State of California has placed additional surtaxes on raw chemical manufacturers as part of its "Green Environment Plan." Metallo management feels that the Industrial product would be better manufactured in Mexico due to more business-friendly regulations. [c] However, Mexico experienced significant inflation in the year 2000 [d] and there is a risk that the Mexican economy could experience significant inflation in the next few years. The location in California would remain a sales distribution point for product to the west coast and provide administrative support to the Mexican facility. [e]

R — regulations — future interco

a. FA + TAX sales division ↓ separate legal entities

As a result, Metallo is wondering whether its sales divisions should be established as separate legal entities, which would be 100% owned as subsidiaries of Metallo. Since the location in Mexico will bear the bulk of the costs associated with manufacturing location changes, Metallo plans to provide assistance to that new subsidiary. Metallo can either provide a loan for a sufficient amount denominated in pesos, or that subsidiary can purchase the needed equipment in Mexico. Megan has been asked to report on any financial accounting and tax implications of such a structural change from divisions to subsidiaries. The U.S., Mexican, and Canadian divisional income statements are provided in Exhibits 4-3, 4-4, and 4-5, respectively.

future interco loan?

assistance ⟶ financing

---

a You will note that the following text is divided into two parts: "Divisional structure" and "Financial statement audit". These parts correspond respectively to Parts "a." and "b." of the "Required" elements. Noticing this association during the reading of the case allows for a better planning of the structure of the response.

b One must be conscious of the fact that an employer or client is sometimes too optimistic. Exhibit a healthy dose of professional scepticism and DO NOT CONFUSE REALITY WITH PROBABILITY.

c This is the second time that the organization is considering the transfer of manufacturing to Mexico due to the less stringent regulations of this country. The ethical consideration of this behaviour must, therefore, be tackled in the response.

d As such, the fact that there was "significant inflation" in 2000 is not an item to be considered since this happened several years ago. Rather, it is the risk that it might reoccur in the future which is relevant, as indicated in the following sentence: "... there is a risk that the Mexican economy could experience significant inflation in the next years".

e The case regularly raises the issue of intercompany transactions, both current and future. In the consideration of that which is Required, the repetition of the presence of the transactions must draw your attention. It is, therefore, useful to identify them as you read in order to be able to quickly return to them while you are drafting.

b. *2. Financial statement audit*

[European interest]

AJX's board of directors recently received an unsolicited offer from a European interest wishing to purchase Metallo. *a* In 2008 and prior years, a separate audit report was not provided for Metallo, although its records were examined during the audit of AJX's consolidated financial statements by its audit firm, Penderson International Auditors. The board has been contacted by the European buyers to obtain Metallo's financial statements, prepared in accordance with International Financial Reporting Standards (IFRS) and audited by a firm other than AJX's auditor. AJX's board has asked Megan to contact audit firms that might be willing to act as independent auditors *b* for Metallo only. Even though the board has decided not to accept the offer at this time, it would like to know how Metallo's financial statements and income taxes will be affected by reporting under IFRS.

[ethic]

[b. FA + TAX affected by reporting under IFRS]

[b. significant changes?]

Megan contacted John, an audit manager from ALN Canada, and arranged the meeting. Megan had met John when he was working on the audit of AJX in 2008 as audit manager for Penderson. *c* At the recent meeting, Megan gave John a copy of the nonconsolidated, unaudited financial statements of Metallo for November 30, 2010 (Exhibit 4-2), along with the three divisional income statements (Exhibits 4-3, 4-4, and 4-5). Megan asked John if, in his view, the non-consolidated financial statements would require significant changes to be presented according to IFRS.

[info given to John early Dec, 10]

Required *d*

[John: 2008 → Penderson → AJX's auditor]
[2010 → ALN → other auditor]

a. Write Megan's letter to AJX's board of directors, discussing the financial accounting and tax issues that might be involved in creating separate subsidiaries. Also make recommendations on the other issues raised, *e* including reporting periods for subsidiaries, risks associated with relocating the manufacturing of the products, and the assistance Metallo can provide to the future subsidiary in Mexico. Your letter should be between 900 and 1,200 words. Your letter should only discuss the issues in principle; you are not required to give direct citations from the *CICA Handbook* and IFRS codes.

[ROLE: external consultant]

[900/1500]

b. Megan has asked John Legg to draft a letter to AJX's board of directors explaining the requirements to revise the financial statements of Metallo in accordance with IFRS and upcoming audit. Write the letter to AJX's board of directors. Your letter should be between 600 and 800 words. Discuss only the issues in principle; you are not required to give direct citations from the *CICA Handbook* and IFRS codes.

[ROLE: external auditor]

---

a The fact that an European interest wishes to purchase Metallo, and not AJX in its entirety, or even AJXFSI, must be identified in order to adequately orient the discussion.

b The notion of "independence" is important for the potential European buyers.

c Personally, once I have read the case the first time around, John's position vis-à-vis AJX did not appear clearly to me. If this also happens to you, take the time to draw a small diagram, such as the one above, in order to ensure that you fully understand what is going on before commencing the resolution of the case.

d One of the peculiarities of the AJX case is that it asks you to play two different roles. Under a., you are MEGAN, an external accountant for several years. In b., you are JOHN, an external audit manager. Although the two letters you are asked to write are directed to the Board of directors, you must pay particular attention to the classification of the various problems or issues to be resolved. Indeed, the angle from which they are to be resolved varies in light of the role you are asked to play. Obviously, the signature at the bottom of each of the letters will have to be different in order to demonstrate your understanding of that which is "Required".

e The Required element asks you to "... make recommendations on the other issues raised", including three specific issues. One must, therefore, pay attention to other problems or issues than those directly mentioned in the Required section. Indeed, one must seek out these "other issues", but one must also remember that they must however arise from the case facts, in light of the case parameters. It would be pointless to consider discussing general topics, without direct links to the particulars of the current case.

Exhibit A – Ajax Metals

EXHIBIT 4-2 _____

METALLO INC.
Statement of Income and Retained Earnings (Unaudited)
year ended November 30, 2010 (in $000s)

	2010	2009
Revenue	$ 102,346	$ 100,138
Cost of goods sold	63,360	62,092
Gross margin	38,986	38,046
Operating expenses		
Selling and distribution	2,560	2,594
Other operating	1,100	1,096
Earnings from operations	35,326	34,356
Financing and administration	30,704	30,042
Foreign exchange gains (losses)	(1,200)	1,000
Earnings before income taxes	3,422	5,314
Income taxes	1,848	1,726
Net earnings	1,574	3,588
Retained earnings, beginning of year	9,628	7,084
Dividends	(242)	(1,044)
Retained earnings, end of year	$ 10,960	$ 9,628

Handwritten notes: Revenue ↑ Earnings ↓ ; 38% (Gross margin); R (Foreign exchange); G/L ↓ (2,200) ! ; Earnings ↓ (2,000) ; ↓ (Dividends)

METALLO INC.
Balance Sheet (Unaudited)
November 30, 2010
(in $000s)

	2010	2009
Assets		
Current assets		
Cash and cash equivalents	$ —	$ 1,676
Short-term investments	—	2,284
Accounts receivable	9,522	8,832
Inventory	10,486	10,380
Prepaid expenses and other current assets	1,886	1,634
	21,894	24,806
Property, plant, and equipment (net)	29,892	21,220
Total assets	$ 51,786	$ 46,026
Liabilities		
Current liabilities		
Current operating loan	$ 6,914	$ 5,392
Accounts payable and accruals	6,668	5,878
Accrued compensation benefits	4,516	3,986
Income taxes payable	2,056	820
Current portion of long-term debt	1,534	788
	21,688	16,864
Long-term debt	9,436	10,276
Future income taxes	6,404	5,960
Total liabilities	$ 37,528	$ 33,100

Handwritten notes: IMP RISK ; negative cash flow +++ ; IMP ↓ WC ratio ; few LT debt

EXHIBIT 4-2 (Continued) *a*

Shareholders' equity

Common shares	$ 3,298	$ 3,298
Retained earnings	10,960	9,628
Total equity	14,258	12,926
Total liabilities and equity	$ 51,786	$ 46,026

METALLO INC. *b*
Cash Flow Statement (Unaudited)
year ended November 30, 2010
(in $000s)

	2010	2009
Operating activities		
Net earnings	$ 1,574	$ 3,588
Amortization of property, plant, and equipment	2,718	1,778
Increase in future income taxes	444	320
Net increase in receivables, inventories, and prepaid expenses	(1048)	(420)
Net increase in accounts payable, accruals, accrued compensation benefits, and taxes payable	2,556	650
Net cash provided by (used by) operating activities	6,244 *OK*	5,916
Investing activities		
Decrease (increase) in short-term investments	2,284	(676)
Additions to property, plant, and equipment	(11,390)	(3,076)
Net cash used by investing activities	(9,106)	(3,752)
Financing activities		
Increase (decrease) in operating loan	1,522	(264)
Repayments of long-term debt	(94)	(1,484)
Cash dividends paid	(242)	(1,044)
Net cash used by financing activities	1,186	(2,792)
Increase (decrease) in cash	(1,676)	(628)
Cash and cash equivalents, beginning of year	1,676	2,304
Cash and cash equivalents, end of year	$ —	$ 1,676

cash flow problem +++

---

a The AJX case includes four pages of financial information. At this point, in light of the restricted time frame of a case, the challenge you face is to quickly flesh out that which may be useful in the drafting of the response.
   When analyzing financial statements provided in a case, one must consider the most significant items (in terms of percentage, variations, and risk), patterns, relationships, and trends, unusual items, inconsistencies and contradictions, non-compliance with accounting standards, laws or business policies, key ratios (more especially those of interest to a creditor or to management), etc.

b It is rather rare that the financial statements supplied in a case include the "Cash Flow Statement". One must, therefore, pay slightly more attention to the case facts contained therein. Since the "cash flow problem" is a primary issue in the AJX case, one can, during the reading stage, flag this importance by placing an appropriate sign, such as "+++".

EXHIBIT 4-2 (Continued)

METALLO INC.
Notes to the Financial Statements (Unaudited)
year ended November 30, 2010
(all amounts in $000s except number of shares)

1. Significant accounting policies

   a. All foreign currency transactions are translated into Canadian dollars at the rate in effect on the date the transaction takes place. *OK*

   b. Inventory is valued at the lower of cost and net realizable value, with cost being determined on a weighted-average basis. *OK*

   b. IFRS fair value?

   c. Property, plant, and equipment is recorded at cost, and amortized over the estimated useful life of the asset at the following rates and methods:

   - Manufacturing plant and equipment: Units of production ($2.80/unit)
   - Automotive equipment: Kilometres driven ($0.50/km)
   - All other equipment: Straight-line (10 years)

2. Inventory

Raw materials	$ 10,198
Work in progress	250
Finished goods	38
Total	$ 10,486

3. Property, plant, and equipment

	Cost	Accumulated Depreciation	Net Book Value — 2010	Net Book Value — 2009
Land	$ 3,650	$ —	$ 3,650	$ 3,650
Manufacturing plant and equipment	37,966	13,120	24,846	16,064
Automotive equipment	362	144	218	266
Other equipment	2,480	1,302	1,178	1,240
Total	$ 44,458	$ 14,566	$ 29,892	$ 21,220

4. Long-term debt

   This loan is entirely payable to AJX Financial Services Inc. Interest and other service fees are payable monthly at rates determined by the common parent company, AJX Inc.

   interco

   b. IFRS rel part

5. Share capital details

   An unlimited number of common voting shares are authorized. The company has 16,490 shares issued and outstanding.

6. Related-party transactions

   A portion of the accounts payable is due to a related party (AJXFSI).

EXHIBIT 4-3 *a*_____

METALLO INC.
U.S. Segment Income Statement
Industrial Product
year ended November 30, 2010
(in 000s, Canadian dollars)

	2010	2009
Revenue	$ 57,600	$ 52,736
Cost of goods sold	34,560	31,642
Gross margin	*40%* $ 23,040	$ 21,094

EXHIBIT 4-4_____

METALLO INC. *b*
Mexico Segment Income Statement
Liquified Product
year ended June 30, 2010 [1]
(in 000s, Canadian dollars)

a. reporting period subs

steady profit level? not really!

	2010	2009
Revenue	$ 17,840	$ 21,782
Cost of goods sold	16,700	20,474
Gross margin	*6%* $ 1,140	$ 1,308

b. audit
- acct system failure
- backups for data

[1] The financial accounting system failed, and the backups for data starting July 1 have not yet been located. The 2010 column is for the reporting period form December 1, 2009 to June 30, 2010.

5 M left

EXHIBIT 4-5_____

METALLO INC.
Canada Segment Income Statement
Standard Product
year ended November 30, 2010
(in 000s, Canadian dollars)

a. relocation

	2010	2009
Revenue	$ 24,200	$ 24,852
Cost of goods sold	16,704	14,876
Gross margin	*31%* $ 7,496	$ 9,976

_____

a The fact that the information is presented per division is a hint in and of itself. One must consider making comparisons.
Also, the fact that the "year ended" is different for the Mexico division must be noted, among others because the "Required" section raises the issue of the reporting periods for subsidiaries.
At a glance, one sees quite clearly that the profitability greatly varies from one division to the next. The Mexico division, in particular, is quite weak. It is, therefore, appropriate to calculate the percentage of gross margin for discussion purposes.

b One must read the case until the very end! A careful reading of this page reveals two problems or issues not mentioned in the previous text, such as the "Profitability of each product" and the "Reliability of the backup system".
Note as well that a note is provided along with the income statement of the Mexico division, although there is none for the others, which should draw your attention.

Exhibit A – Ajax Metals

CONTEXT
→ public → IFRS
→ international supplier
→ chemicals (risk) (3 types)
→ AJX mgmt/BOD monitor
→ constraint: near capacity
→ strength: inventory is minimal
→ STRAT: managing supply on markets
→ steady profit level
→ threath: regulated environment
→ obj.: MAX deductions to lower taxable income

SEPARATE SUBS - ACCT
- consolidation
- interco (+++)
   US subs / MX subs
   Metallo / subs (loan)
- foreign currency

REPORTING PERIOD SUBS
- inflation MX
- June / Nov
- missing data

SEPARATE SUBS - TAX
- interco
   AJXFSI (FMV?)
- countries → rates/rules
- purchase/lease equipment (IMP)

RISKS RELOCATING
- agric. uncertain
- inflation MX
+++ - negative cash flow ($)
- profitability ? ($)
+/- - financing (loan) ($)

ASSISTANCE
METALLO MX
- missing data (backups)
?

a.

REVISE FS → IFRS
- inflation MX (+++)
- consolidation
- foreign currency
- related parties (+++)

REPORTING PERIOD SUBS
- acceptance
- missing data
- GOING CONCERN (+++)

b.

ETHIC
a. relocating :
   cosmetic US → MX
   industrial CA → MX

b. upcoming audit
   • independence

---

a   Since it is a worksheet for the exclusive use of its author, the contents vary from one person to the next in light of one's requirements and of the particulars of the case.
Of course, the words can and MUST BE FURTHER ABBREVIATED since time is running. What is important is to be able to quickly and easily find one's bearings. For instance, "FX" may very well be a substitute for the words "Foreign currency". You will surely understand that, for the purposes of this volume, I wish to present the text clearly. One must, however, make sure to retain the significant words in the Required elements, such as "risks relocating", in order to constantly keep in mind the direction in which the response is heading. In this case, one will be required to discuss the "risks associated with relocating", and not the risks which the organization is facing in general.

Suggested Solution *a*

Part a

Megan Jones, CGA
42 Love Street
Toronto, Ontario N4B 1M1

December 15, 2010

Board of Directors, AJX Inc.
62 Industrial Park Way
Regina, SK

Subject: Organizational Structure of Metallo *b*

Dear Directors:

Thank you for the opportunity to discuss some of the financial and tax issues related to creating separate subsidiaries.

Creating separate subsidiaries - ACCT

Currently, the U.S. and Mexico divisions are sales divisions, selling products exclusively from Metallo. The price structure and all decisions are made by Metallo or AJX. The financial reporting for divisions is much simpler than that of consolidating subsidiaries.

Consolidation

If Metallo were to incorporate the U.S. and Mexico divisions as wholly owned subsidiaries, these companies' financial results would need to be consolidated with that of Metallo's. Consideration would need to be given to consolidation methods, eliminating inter-company transactions, and foreign currency translations.

Foreign currency translation

Since the foreign subsidiaries will be financially and operationally dependent, they will need to translate the financial statement using the foreign currency transaction approach. This method reports the foreign subsidiary's financial activities as if they were carried out as an integral part of the parent's operations rather than as a separate entity. Translation gains and losses arising from monetary items must be included in the determination of net income, whether the business structure is continued as divisions or subsidiaries. The equipment to be purchased in Mexico can be recorded at cost using the spot rate in effect on that date, resulting in no exchange gains or losses at balance sheet date because it is a non-monetary item. Currently, it is not required to be recorded at market value. If a decision is made in the future to carry the equipment at market value, the exchange rate in effect at the balance sheet date will be used for translation, resulting in gains or losses.

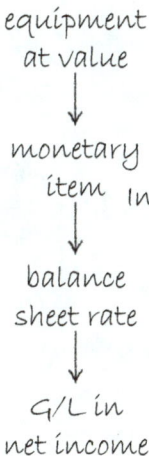

Intercompany transactions

In preparing the consolidated statements, it will be important that all inter-company transactions between Metallo and its subsidiaries be tracked and eliminated (for example, the potential loan from Metallo to a Mexican subsidiary) and only transactions with external entities remain. *c*

_____

a In this suggested solution, the case facts are highlighted in yellow, whereas the theoretical concepts are highlighted in green. Comments that you could write down during the analysis of this suggested solution are written in the font used here. The following abbreviations: "P" (identification of problem/issue), "I" (impact, consequences), and "R" or "REC" (recommendation) are used frequently.

b Since the solution takes the form of an uninterrupted text, I suggest that you identify the problems or issues discussed – which appear here as headings – in order to better show the structure of the suggested solution.

c This paragraph is a model of drafting which should be emulated. The theoretical concepts are integrated simultaneously with the case facts.

Margin notes (right side):

ASPE
↓
3061.04
↓
Cost model

equipment
at cost
↓
non-
monetary
item
↓
historical
rate
↓
no exchange
G/L

Margin notes (left side):

equipment
at value
↓
monetary
item
↓
balance
sheet rate
↓
G/L in
net income

Handwritten note (top right):

Since the "Required" elements ask you to draft a letter, you must present your response in this form, and not forget to include your signature at the end (A13). The letterhead could, however, be succinct. What is important is that the sections DATE, TO, FROM, SUBJECT appears in your response.

1- reporting date

2- significant inflation

To be compliant with IFRS (*CICA Handbook* — Part I), the reporting date must coincide for all the subsidiaries or divisions. The transactions between July 1 and November 30 must be recorded for the Mexican division to make the information reliable. If a subsidiary is established with a differing fiscal period than that of Metallo, those transactions must be disclosed or recorded as appropriate. Another issue exists due to the potential that Mexico may experience significant inflation. IFRS requires the restatement of prior periods to current currency values for comparability. a

IAS 29.08   comparability concept

As mentioned on page A15, the restatement of prior periods is not a requirement under current standards (ASPE).

Creating separate subsidiaries - TAX

Regarding the lost data in Mexico, it is essential to have policies and procedures in place for backup and recovery at each location (for example, disk mirroring). These must be established prior to any modifications to the business structure. Ensure, at the very least, that a copy of data is submitted from each location on a regular basis, preferably daily.

when   *practical aspect*

link between the accounting issue and the tax issue

For income tax purposes, each foreign division will have income tax obligations to the country in which it is located. Thus, each subsidiary will need to produce its own financial statements that reflect the earnings that occur within each country. Goods and services will need to be transferred at fair market values in order to ensure that the proper tax is paid in each country. Although these transactions are eliminated when preparing the consolidated statements, it is the separate entity statements that will be used for income tax determinations. It would be prudent to examine the tax rates in each country to determine whether some functions should be performed in the countries with the lowest tax rates; however, this must be the result of actual operations, not just a transferring of revenues and expenses beyond fair values in order to manipulate tax payments. b

Be cautious in your advice!

Planning? YES

Manipulating? NO

Intercompany transactions

tax point of view

Furthermore, the fees currently paid to AJXFSI may be disallowed in the event of a tax audit because they could be considered excessive for the services provided and may be considered only to exist to transfer income to a tax haven. This could result in a possible contingent liability for a significant tax reassessment. Ensure that the underlying agreement between Metallo and AJXFSI supports the fees charged. These international tax issues are complex and frequently changing. I would advise that an international tax expert be consulted on these issues.   *Be careful whit a tax haven!*

Leasing or purchasing the equipment

specific tax rules

Either leasing or purchasing the equipment for the Ontario location will result in allowable tax deductions. Quantitative amounts will need to be provided in order to determine if capital cost allowance deductions on owned equipment will be higher than leasing. It appears the equipment will qualify for Class 29. You can elect to place in Class 29 eligible machinery and equipment acquired after March 18, 2007 and before 2012 that would otherwise be included in Class 43. To make an election, a letter needs to be attached to the income tax return for the tax year the property is bought indicating that you are electing to put the property in Class 29. CCA is calculated using the straight line method as follows: claim up to 25% in the first year, 50% in the second year, and the remaining 25% in the third year. Finally, leasing costs are deducted in the year they were incurred, while CCA is an optional deduction that may be saved for future years when there is taxable income that needs to be reduced. c

WHEN + HOW MUCH

tax planning

LEASING	PURCHASING
allowable tax deduction	allowable tax deduction
deducted in the year incurred	CCA - Class 29 - 25% - 50% - 25%
mandatory	optional

or Class 43: 30%

a One notes that the discussion of the accounting issues precedes that of the tax issues. This is a logical sequencing of the issues, since it is generally easier to discuss the tax treatment once the transaction has been adequately recorded in the books.

b One also notes that the "accounting" and "taxation" issues are discussed separately. This manner of proceeding ought to be emulated. Too often, it happens that candidates discuss the two aspects together in a jumbled manner. The discussion is often harder to follow, which complicates the task of the assessor who must assess the depth of analysis of each of the issues. It is generally preferable to separate the topics (and subtopics), and to present clear connections between the two a little later on, such as the difference in the accounting treatment and tax treatment of the intercompany transactions.

c Please note that, since the publication of the AJX case by CGA-Canada, the availability of Class 29 was extended to 2014.

© CGA = COMPETENCY

Risks associated with relocating the manufacturing of the products

In determining whether it is appropriate to relocate some of the manufacturing, a thorough risk analysis of each location and profitability of each product must be conducted. Overall, Metallo is experiencing a cash flow problem, which may increase with some of the proposed changes. Industrial ranks as the most profitable, with a 40% gross margin, followed by Standard, at 31%, then Liquified, with 6%. [a] There is a risk of inflation in Mexico. Investing in that location as inflation rises may lead to increased costs for the group overall, further reducing cash flows. While Industrial appears to be the most profitable, Metallo should consider additional testing, in light of the California study, before continuing and moving production to Mexico. Furthermore, Metallo's public image may be tarnished should the health concerns over Industrial continue to spread, including the possibility of potential lawsuits against Metallo.

clear conclusions

cost/benefit concept

cost/benefit to relocate:
- profitability
- cash flow problem
- inflation
- public image

Supplying agricultural producers

Supplying agricultural producers with the product and packaging required for retail sales of the Liquified product likely violates Ontario regulations and therefore has serious potential to damage Metallo's reputation. Since Liquified is the least profitable product, it is not recommended to relocate this product to Ontario, given the risks associated. In considering the risks and profitability associated with Standard, it may be feasible to continue production in Mexico; however, a full analysis of the risks should be undertaken. If the production of Standard is moved to Mexico without the reciprocal move of Liquified production to Ontario, then the Canadian manufacturing plant would need to be shut down. The impact on the community and the other social costs of shutting this facility down should be assessed.

violation of regulations → reputation

Assistance Metallo can provide: Financing

3 divisions → 3 recommendations

At this point, I recommend that financing should be made available to Metallo from AJXFSI and that relocations only occur after thorough studies regarding each location are conducted. The financing must be matched to the cash requirements — short term for operations and long term for capital investments. It appears that the recent investment in equipment was financed through short-term funds, which seems to have caused the cash shortage. I hope this has provided you with the advice required.

justified recommendations

Yours truly,

Megan Jones, CGA

short and sweet signature

actual cash flow problem
+
- proposed changes
- risk of inflation
=
future cash flow problem

chemical manufacturing
↓
health concerns
↓
potential lawsuits

KEY DECISION FACTORS: PROFITABILITY + RISKS

ACTUAL SITUATION	CHANGES PROPOSED BY METALLO	SUGGESTED SOLUTION
CA - Standard / cosmetic	relocate in Mx	• relocate in Mexico • shut down CA plant
MX - Liquified / agriculture	relocate in CA	• not recommended to relocate in CA Ontario
US - Industrial / plastic	relocate in Mx	• consider additional testing before relocate in MX

[a] Since the calculation of the gross margin of each of the divisions is short, it can very easily be incorporated into the text itself. It is, therefore, not necessary to create an Exhibit as such. Personally, at least for one of the three divisions, I would have presented the source of the % obtained in brackets, as follows, for the Industrial division: 40% (23,043/57,600).

Part b
ALN Canada
John Legg, CGA
426 Dove Street
Toronto, Ontario N4B 1L1

Required:

"explaining the requirements to revise the financial statements of Metallo in accordance with IFRS"

December 16, 2010

Board of Directors, AJX Inc.
62 Industrial Park Way
Regina, SK

Since the "Required" elements ask you to draft a letter, you must present your response in this form, and not forget to include your signature at the end (A15). The letterhead could, however, be succinct. What is important is that the sections DATE, TO, FROM, SUBJECT appears in your response.

Subject: Financial Statements and Related Issues

Dear Directors:

Thank you for considering ALN Canada to undertake the audit of Metallo's financial statements for the 2010 year end. In our meeting with your accountant, Megan Jones, a number of questions were raised that we would like to address. *a*

Metallo financial statements   *One must compare ASPE/IFRS.*

justified REC

AJX^R must adopt IFRS for January 2011 because it is publicly traded, but earlier adoption is permitted. To be consistent with AJX and facilitate the consolidation process, it is^R recommended that Metallo adopt IFRS for this fiscal year. The statements for the fiscal year ending November 30, 2009 would then have to be restated to IFRS for comparative purposes. An opening IFRS statement of financial position at the date of transition to IFRS will have to be prepared.   *IFRS 1*   *choice for Metallo: ASPE or IFRS*

There are many examples of similarities and differences between pre IFRS GAAP standards and current GAAP standards The following highlights some key differences and similarities: *a*

Financial statements concepts
The underlying concepts are very similar — financial statements^R must be understandable, relevant, and reliable. Business combinations are treated very similarly under both sets of principles.

similarity: business combinations

Disclosures and related parties
An example of differences that can impact Metallo's reporting is the requirement for disclosure of segment liabilities, which is not required in the current *Handbook*. *a*

difference: disclosure of segment liabilities

You have provided disclosure of some related-party transactions; however, the disclosure must be much more detailed. Examples of further disclosure requirements follow: *difference: disclosure of related-party transactions*

The requirements of IAS 24.18 are illustrated using the intercompany transactions referred to in the case.

- All transactions between Metallo and AJX Inc/AJXFSI
- The amount of any accounts receivable and accounts payable between Metallo and AJX/AJXFSI
- Fees paid to AJX/AJXFSI and key management personnel IAS 24.17
- An explanation of how the transition from previous GAAP to IFRS affected Metallo's reported financial position, performance, and cash flows IFRS 1.23
- The entire long-term debt payable to AJXFSI and terms of repayment
- The nature of the relationship with any related parties there have been transactions with IAS 24.13

While this list is not all-inclusive, it does indicate how IFRS disclosures are much more detailed than those required for pre-changeover GAAP. *b*

---

a This introduction could be drafted in a more succinct manner. Under circumstances where the time allotted for the drafting of the case is restricted, one must tackle the resolution of the problems or issues as soon as possible.

b It is not necessary to repeat, word for word, the wording of IAS 24. What is important is to adequately present, in an integrated manner, the relevant concepts.

Foreign currency translation

similarity: treatment of foreign division

justified procedure assertion: accuracy

It appears that the ongoing transactions of Metallo's foreign divisions are being treated correctly, resulting in exchange gains or losses included in net income. We will need to R examine the foreign currency exchange rates that have been used to ensure that they are accurate and consistent.

difference: excessive inflation context

Also, in the event that Metallo does invest in a subsidiary in Mexico, and excessive inflation occurs, IAS 29 requires restatement of financial statements due to hyperinflation. This is not a requirement under current standards. Hyperinflation has its main effect on monetary assets and liabilities. Any equipment purchased in Mexican pesos is considered to be a non-monetary item. [a]

2 solutions:
- retrieve the backup
OR
- reconstruct the data

The audit of Metallo financial statements [b]

At this point: POTENTIAL

Missing information issue

ST

Presently, the lack of information for the Mexico division can create a potential scope limitation. We must R obtain evidence for the period from July 1 to November 30. This may be avoided if staff can successfully ✓ retrieve the backup or ✓ reconstruct the data. Failing this, and should the scope limitation prove to be material, a qualification of our opinion can result. I would R recommend that appropriate controls be implemented to avoid future occurrences.

LT

Going concern issue

difference: audit work concerning going concern

cash flow problem → going concern issue → more evidence to obtain

Since the reporting period ends November 30, 2010, Metallo is not subject to examination under the Canadian Auditing Standards (CAS). These standards must be applied for audits of financial statements for periods ending on or after December 14, 2010. While many of the standards are the same between Canadian GAAS and CAS, there is a difference that can potentially impact future audits. Currently, Metallo is experiencing cash flow problems. While this seems to have occurred in the last year due to a mismatching of financing with investment, risk-assessment procedures must be conducted to determine if management's assumption for a going concern is valid. There must be adequate disclosure of any material uncertainty regarding the ability of Metallo to realize its assets and discharge its liabilities. Even with adequate disclosure, under CAS, we must include an emphasis of matter paragraph in our report. This is a significant difference from the current reporting standard.

clear conclusion

CAS 570.12

CAS 570.18

CAS 570.19

Independence

case facts used to justify the independence issue

Megan has indicated that your interest in Metallo's audit is to obtain independent assurance on the financial accuracy of Metallo's separate entity financial statements that the potential buyers can rely upon. I have considered my perceived independence. As a previous employee of Penderson, AJX's audit firm, I acted as audit manager in 2008. While I believe that as a CGA I can, in fact, conduct the audit objectively, the potential buyers may perceive otherwise. Therefore, in order to ensure that the parties' request is honoured, R I must remove myself from this engagement as audit manager. Consequently, I will R recommend another audit manager within our firm to conduct this engagement so as to not compromise independence, either in fact or in appearance for the interested parties.

stakeholders requirement considered

justified REC

Thank you for the opportunity of service. We look forward to providing further assistance in the future.

independence / perceived conflict of interest concepts

Yours truly,

John Legg, CGA

---

a Since the context of the drafting of the letter to be written under b. is different from that under a., it is normal to observe a certain repetition of the topics. Take, for instance, the case fact that Mexico could experience significant inflation. Under a., this is a "risk associated with the relocation of the products in Mexico". Under b., this is a requirement "to revise the financial statements in accordance with IFRS". The "significant inflation" is the same case fact but used in two different contexts.

b In general, the discussion of the accounting issues precedes that of the audit issues. This is a logical sequencing of the issues since it is easier to discuss implications regarding the upcoming audit once the adjustments to the financial statements have been previously discussed.

Required: "discussing financial accounting that might be involved in creating separate subsidiaries"

Competency Grids a

Part a

directed question ↓ *explicit answer*

Core and core-related competencies   A11   FA: Financial accounting

PK:FA:03 — Researches, evaluates, and advises on the appropriate accounting treatment for complex transactions (step-by-step acquisitions, fair value determinations, encumbrances, endowment trusts, financial instruments)

Baseline question: Did the candidate explain the differences between subsidiaries and sales divisions and the accounting issues for subsidiaries or segments of Metallo?

focus: separate entities or not

ASPE

Performance level	Solution Key
0. *NR/Inc* [1]	Did not attempt or insufficient response to evaluate, OR incorrect
1. *Substantially below*	**Identified** that: ☐ Subsidiaries are separate entities. ☐ Sales divisions are not separate entities.
2. *Below*	**Discussed** that: ☐ Metallo's reporting requirements will become more complex for subsidiaries contrasted to divisions. ☐ Reporting of foreign currency gains and losses will change. ☐ Intercompany transactions of sales and purchases must be eliminated. ☐ Other
3. *Meets*	**Discussed AND explained:** ☐ How the intercompany transactions will be eliminated. HOW ☐ That only transactions with external parties will remain after elimination of intercompany transactions. ☐ There is a difference in reporting foreign currency denominated monetary (loan) and long-term non-monetary (equipment) items. ☐ The type of subsidiaries that may be created and whether they are integrated or self-sustaining. ☐ If the organization changes the structure of its segments, the disclosures for prior periods must be restated. ☐ Other
4. *Exceeds*	**Discussed AND explained** the available data and information **AND made a recommendation** supported by the analysis, including the following: ☐ The loan by Metallo to the Mexico subsidiary will be eliminated on consolidation. ☐ Equipment will be recorded at the spot rate in effect on the date it is purchased. ☐ There will be no exchange gains or losses recognized on the equipment because it is a non-monetary item. ☐ Other

basic ideas

clear financial accounting concepts

The use of brackets allows you to quickly show case integration.

At the "Exceeds" level, one notes the use of case facts in the drafting of each of the recommendations.

[1] NR = No Response; Inc = Incorrect

"Other" valid point: "The subsidiaries are integrated because AJX/Metallo monitor the decisions and activities."

THE CONTEXT OF THE DISCUSSION IS IMPORTANT.

One must discuss "financial accounting", that is to say the presentation of the transactions in the external financial statements. And, from this point of view, creating separate entities is causing differences. However, for the purposes of internal management, the implications of this change are limited since AJX may achieve the same internal reporting, whether of the manufacturing sales division or of the subsidiaries. Note, however, that this latter comment, although true, is not part of the response to this case. It is quite simply not Required!

a *In the current Competency Grids, the case facts are highlighted in yellow, whereas the theoretical concepts are highlighted in green. Comments that you could write down when analyzing this grid are written in the font used here.*

Competency Grids (continued)

Core and core-related competencies _A12_   _FA: Financial accounting_

PK:FA:06 — Ensures the preparation of timely, reliable, and relevant financial information (financial system design, quality control systems for financial reporting, internal controls)

Baseline question: Did the candidate explain the issue concerning the different reporting period end dates and explain the need for timely, reliable information from Metallo's reporting units?

ISSUE
"reporting periods for subs" ↓

ANALYSIS
"discussed and explained" ↓

RECOMMEND

Performance level	Solution Key
0. _NR/Inc_	Did not attempt or insufficient response to evaluate, OR incorrect
1. _Substantially below_	**Identified** that: ☐ The reporting period end date for the division in Mexico does not coincide with the reporting period for Metallo.
2. _Below_ _Mexico: June 30_ _Others: Nov 30_	**Discussed** that: ☐ To be GAAP/IFRS compliant, the reporting date for all subsidiaries/divisions must coincide. ☐ The schedule for the Mexican division does not report for an entire accounting period. ☐ Other
3. _Meets_	**Discussed AND explained:** ☐ How the time period principle has been violated. _HOW_ ☐ The users cannot make valid business decisions because the Mexican division information is not timely. ☐ Due to the potential of significant inflation in Mexico, IFRS[R] requires in the restatement of prior periods to current currency values for comparability. ☐ Other
4. _Exceeds_ _recommendations justified with case facts_	**Discussed AND explained** the available data and information **AND made a recommendation** supported by the analysis, including the following: ☐ The transactions between July 1 and November 30 for the Mexican division need to be recorded. ☐ If a Mexican subsidiary is established with a fiscal period different than that of Metallo's, those transactions must be disclosed or recorded as appropriate. ☐ Other

7 months instead of 12

user's needs concept

comparability concept

In order to properly respond to the "Required" elements, one must have noticed two things: That the year ended of the divisions does not coincide AND that there are five months of operations missing from Mexico. A close examination of Exhibits 4-3, 4-4 and 4-5 allows you to flesh out the information necessary to the resolution of this issue. One must, therefore, take the time to read the entire case before beginning the drafting phase, and I do mean until the last word!

The topics of financial accounting to be discussed under the Required a. section are specifically set out: "Creating separate subsidiaries" (A16) and "Reporting period for subsidiaries" (A17). On the other hand, under the Required b. section, the request is broader: "Revise the financial statements in accordance with IFRS" (A27).

Under a., the depth of analysis of each of the two topics requested is sought.

Under b., what is sought instead is the breadth of differences/similarities between ASPE and IFRS.

Exhibit A – Ajax Metals

Required: "discussing tax issues that might be involved in creating separate subsidiaries"

Competency Grids (continued)

A12

Core and core-related competencies   TX: Taxation

PK:TX:02 — Determines and advises on taxpayer's tax liability (taxes related to income, consumption, payroll, property)

Baseline question: Did the candidate explain the different tax treatments between subsidiaries and sales divisions and explain that the subsidiaries will be separate entities that have their own tax obligations apart from Metallo?

focus: separate entities or not

1- The subsidiaries are separate legal entities.

2- The entities transact amongst themselves.

3- The entities are located in different countries.

directed question ↓ explicit answer

Performance level	Solution Key
0. *NR/Inc*	Did not attempt or insufficient response to evaluate, OR incorrect
1. *Substantially below*	**Identified** that: ☐¹ Sales divisions do not directly pay income taxes because divisions are not separate legal entities.
2. *Below*	**Discussed:** ☐¹ Subsidiaries pay income taxes as a legal entity. ☐² There may be transfer pricing issues between Metallo and the subsidiaries. ☐ Other
3. *Meets*	**Discussed AND explained:** ☐³ Subsidiaries will pay income tax based on the tax rates in each country where they are resident. ☐² Goods and services between Metallo and the subsidiaries will need to be transferred at fair market values to ensure proper tax is paid in each country. ☐ Fees currently paid to AJXFSI may be disallowed in the event of a tax audit because they could be considered excessive for the services provided to only transfer income to a tax haven, possibly resulting in contingent liability for a significant tax reassessment. ☐ Other
4. *Exceeds*	**Discussed AND explained** the available data and information **AND made a recommendation** supported by the analysis, including the following: ☐³ An examination of the tax rates in each country must be made to determine which country has the lowest tax rate. ☐³ Lower overall tax may be paid if more income can be earned in the country with the lowest tax rate. ☐² Revenues and expenses cannot be transferred from one subsidiary to another just to manipulate tax payments. ☐² An examination of the underlying agreement between AJXFSI and Metallo must be made to determine the validity of the fees charged. ☐ Other

level 1: basic tax rules

clear tax rules

2- and 3- (handwritten note pointing into Meets row)

At the "Exceeds" level, one must go beyond the explanation of the tax rules and submit a list of actions to take.

One must use the appropriate terms, namely "subsidiary" or "sales division" in order to clearly express the idea.

Be sceptic with a "tax haven"

tax planning

objective: follow tax rules

The fact that "The financing and administration expenses paid to AJXFSI are calculated at 30% of revenue." seems arbitrary. Hence, since this payment in part covers the financing costs, which costs do not generally vary according to the revenue, one must demonstrate the healthy dose of professional scepticism.

International tax issues are beyond our CGA expertise (A26). One must, however, know that one must take into account, generally speaking, the fact that the subsidiaries are located in different countries.

Required: "discussing tax issues that might be involved in creating separate subsidiaries"

Competency Grids (continued)

"Metallo management would like to maximize deductions associated with the equipment to lower the taxable income" (A4)

Core and core-related competencies *A12*   TX: Taxation

PK:TX:08 — Evaluates and advises on tax implications of alternative business decisions (lease versus buy, dividend versus salary, sharing small-business deductions, contract versus employee)

Baseline question: Did the candidate identify and explain the tax implications for equipment purchases or leases?

1- Equipment purchases
2- Equipment leases

focus: tax deductions

Since the decision to purchase or lease the packaging equipment is not yet made, one must discuss the tax implications of the two alternatives. There is certainly more to say about the purchase of the equipment, as opposed to the leasing thereof. However, at the "Meets" level, it appears to me to be essential to demonstrate that one understands the main difference between the two alternatives.

Why is there no pros/cons discussion about purchasing or leasing the equipment? Simply because this is not Required. The client does not ask for it and also, this is a question far removed from the immediate problems and issues.

Quick deduction compared to the usual useful life of an equipment.

Performance level	Solution Key
0. *NR/Inc*	Did not attempt or insufficient response to evaluate, OR incorrect
1. *Substantially below* — *very basic concepts*	**Stated** that: ☐ 1- Capital cost allowance is a deduction to reduce tax liability. ☐ 2- The leasing costs of equipment can be deducted to reduce taxes payable.
2. *Below* — 1- {	**Identified:** ☐ The tax treatment of leasing costs compared to capital cost allowance ☐ Assets are grouped in pools according to type, and deductions are claimed as a percentage of the balance in the pool. ☐ If the previously purchased equipment is sold, the proceeds are deducted from the pool. ☐ New equipment purchases are added to a pool of assets, which are classified according to the *Income Tax Act*. ☐ Other
3. *Meets* — *clear tax rules* 1- { ... 1- and 2-	**Identified AND explained:** ☐ That if the new equipment is the same class as the old equipment, its cost will be entered into that pool. ☐ No terminal loss for the recently purchased equipment can be claimed unless it is the last item in the pool. ☐ Manufacturing equipment generally is included in Class 43. ☐ There are transitional provisions to recognize the different rates for Class 43 depending on when the item was purchased. ☐ Leasing costs are deducted in the current year, but CCA is an optional deduction that can be saved for future years. ☐ Other
4. *Exceeds* — *clear application of tax rules* 1- {	**Identified AND explained** the available data and information **AND made a recommendation** supported by the analysis, including the following: ☐ The equipment qualifies as Class 29 — ME because it is obtained in 2011. ☐ The election needs to be made in the form of a letter and attached to the income tax return. ☐ CCA using the straight line method as follows: claim up to 25% in the first year, 50% in the second year, and the remaining 25% in the third year. ☐ Any amount not claimed in a year can be claimed in a subsequent year. ☐ Other

Without performing the calculation as such, one can see that the deductions allowed pursuant to Class 29 will likely be higher than those arising from the "low monthly leasing payments". Since the objective of management is to maximize deductions to lower the taxable income, one can recommend the purchase since it better meets this objective than leasing.

This would, in my opinion, be another valid point to consider at the "Exceeds" level.

N.B.: The preceding comments remain valid if one considers that Class 43 allows for one to claim 30%.

Exhibit A – Ajax Metals

Required: "Making recommendations on the risks associated with relocating the manufacturing of the products".

— non-directed issue —

Competency Grids (continued)

chemicals manufacturing
↓
environment
↓
public health

A13 **Core and core-related competencies**   ET: Ethics and trust

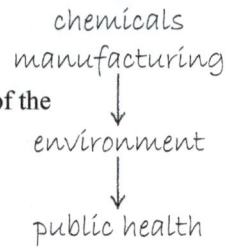

PR:ET:04 — Protects the public interest (maintains and raises the visibility of the ethical nature of the profession and professional accounting standards)

Baseline question: Did the candidate explain there is an ethical issue with moving production of potentially hazardous material (Industrial) from the United States to Mexico in order to avoid the potential public health issue and the regulations in the United States?

It is important to identify the inadequate behaviour of one's client (or of one's employer) and, especially, not to follow suit.

Performance level	Solution Key
0. *NR/Inc*	Did not attempt or insufficient response to evaluate, OR incorrect
1. *Substantially below*	**Restated** the facts of the case without elaboration: ☐ Moving production is to avoid regulation and public health concerns
2. *Below*	**Identified** the issues: ☐ Unethical business practice *conclusion* ☐ Other
3. *Meets*	**Identified AND explained** the impact of moving Industrial from the United States to Mexico: ☐ Public perception of the move ☐ Not in public interest ☐ Appears that Metallo is trying to circumvent the public health concerns in the United States ☐ Other
4. *Exceeds*	**Identified** the issues, **explained** the impact, **AND made a recommendation** supported by the analysis, including the following: ☐ Recommends not to move production ☐ Recommends to discontinue Industrial sales until the public health concerns are addressed ☐ Conduct more tests on product to ensure safety ☐ Plan for scenario where product can no longer be sold due to safety concerns ☐ Other

impact (row 3)

clear recommendations WHAT TO DO (row 4)

One should be prudent where "public health" is concerned.

see beyond the numbers ✓

Since public health is at play, one must take this issue very seriously. Moving manufacturing to a country with more business-friendly regulations does not solve the problem! Indeed, Metallo will be in compliance with the Mexico regulations, but, under certain circumstances, this is not sufficient. Incidentally, one notes that the recommendations set out at the "Exceeds" level are unambiguous: the organization is not allowed to ignore its social responsibilities.

	Standard	Liquified	Industrial
ACTUAL	CA	MX	US
FUTURE	MX	CA	MX

↑   ↑

It is clear that the preservation of public health /safety concerns is very significant. The minimization of the surtaxes on raw chemical manufactures is, therefore, not the only objective to consider.

One should note that Metallo is considering manufacturing the Standard product in Mexico where "no bans on pesticides used for cosmetic purposes" exist. I consider that his relocation plan is also part of this "ethical issue". Since these products are now prohibited for sale in Ontario, it would not be a responsible behaviour to manufacture the same product in Mexico just because this market is readily available! Public health is a concern, no matter where!

Required: "Making recommendations on the assistance Metallo can provide to the future subsidiary in Mexico".

Competency Grids (continued)

A12

Core and core-related competencies   IT: Information technology

PK:IT:02 — Selects and uses appropriate business technology tools in the workplace (spreadsheets, tax compliance software, generalized audit software, online knowledge bases)

Baseline question: Did the candidate discuss the need for a reliable backup system for the location in Mexico and provide relevant advice or solutions to address this concern?

reliable info concept

It is imperative to find means of recovering the data.

Performance level	Solution Key
0. *NR/Inc*	Did not attempt or insufficient response to evaluate, OR incorrect
1. *Substantially below*	**Identified** that: ☐ There is a need to backup data.
2. *Below*	**Described** that: ☐ Backups must be conducted on a regular basis. ☐ Backups should be stored off-site in order to be reliable. ☐ Other
3. *Meets* *key point: restore data*	**Described AND discussed**: ☐ How the backup data can be used to restore the transactions between July 1 and November 30. ☐ There are various methods to backup data which are removable, fixed, or remote. ☐ Other
4. *Exceeds* *solutions*	**Described AND discussed** the available data and information **AND made a recommendation** supported by analysis, including the following: ☐ Prior to establishing a subsidiary in Mexico, there must be policies and procedures established for backup and recovery of data. ☐ Recommended a particular method of backup — remote (Internet), disk mirroring, disk duplexing, etc. for a fault tolerant system. ☐ Recommended that data from each location is submitted on a regular (daily) basis to Metallo's head office. ☐ Other

basic concepts

HOW

priori

posteriori

It is important to place the events on a time line. The recovery of the financial information is a priority.

ONE situation ↓ MULTIPLE impacts

failure of the financial accounting system

A9

+

backups for data starting July 1 have not yet been located

WHEN

One must look for solutions to all the problems raised by the case.

need for timely, reliable information (A17)

need for a reliable backup system (A21)

need to avoid a scope limitation (A29)

Frequently, the consideration of circumstances specific to the case brings about a discussion of more than one issue. Indeed, the implications of this situation can impact more than one aspect of the organization's activities.

The loss of five months of financial data is a significant event which warrants reflection as to the multiple repercussions that flow from it. One must, therefore, not believe THAT A CASE FACT leads to a discussion OF A SINGLE ISSUE.

Required: "Making recommendations on the risks associated with relocating the manufacturing of the products".

Competency Grids (continued)

A13

Core and core-related competencies   BE: Business environment

PK:BE:03 — Anticipates and recognizes market factors and stakeholders' interests, and adapts business decisions and processes

Baseline question: Did the candidate explain the risks associated with restructuring the operations and locations and provide recommendations to minimize the risks? Three issues should be identified.

ISSUE "risks with relocating" ↓

ANALYSIS "discussed and explained" ↓

RECOMMEND

3 divisions ↓ 3 locations ↓ 3 different environments

inflation ↓ cash flow problem ↓ going concern

Performance level	Solution Key
0. *NR/Inc*	Did not attempt or insufficient response to evaluate, OR incorrect
1. *Substantially below*	**Identified** that: ☐ Risks will be **different** in **each location**.

2. *Below*
 	
major risk of each location
	Discussed:
	☐ Risks associated with each location:
	  o **Inflation in Mexico**
	  o Foreign currency risks for **U.S. location and Mexico**
	  o **Legal and regulatory** risks in Ontario and California
	☐ Other

3. *Meets* *IMPACT*	**Discussed AND explained** costs associated with particular risks: ☐ Lawsuits, leading to legal costs ☐ **Moving production locations** ☐ Loss of reputation from potential violation of **regulations in Ontario** ☐ **Inflation in Mexico** can lead to cash flow problems for the overall group. ☐ Cash flow problems can lead to **going concern** issues. ☐ **Investment of new packaging line** may not be profitable in the long term. ☐ Other
4. *Exceeds* *Solutions to mitigate or to eliminate the risks*	**Discussed AND explained** the available data and information **AND made a recommendation** supported by the analysis, including the following: ☐ Obtain further information on the **California study** to determine if production of **this chemical** is warranted in the long term. US ☐ Investigate the regulations to determine if selling the **agricultural product** will violate those regulations. CA ☐ Obtain accurate costs of **leasing and buying the equipment**. MX ☐ Other

3 countries ↓ 3 recommendations

In a business advice context, you should consider the risks.

"Other" valid point: "Conduct a **market study** in order to determine the existence and size of the market prior to transferring production to Ontario."

FOCUS: costs associated/ impact on profitability

All the recommendations provided above start with a verb that uses the imperative or the infinitive form. It forces you to be more specific in determining what action needs to be undertaken.

Personally, in light of the added risks in connection with Metallo's activities, I would have stated a conclusion, namely that the risks associated with restructuring the operations are high.

Required: "Making recommendations on   – non-directed issue –   A23
the risks associated with relocating
the manufacturing of the products".

Competency Grids (continued)

Core and core-related competencies   A13   FN: Finance

PK:FN:07 — Manages cash flow and working capital (sets working capital levels including bank balances, receivable balances, and payable balances; formulates policies for granting credit to customers and making payments to suppliers; hedges market risks — interest rates, foreign exchange, commodity risks)

Baseline question: Did the candidate discuss the need to closely monitor cash flow prior to making decisions regarding relocation and asset purchases, and analyze and recommend options to achieve these business goals?

insufficient CASH

↓

jeopardized INVESTMENT
- relocations
- equipment

↓

FINANCING solutions

Performance level	Solution Key
0. NR/Inc	Did not attempt or insufficient response to evaluate, OR incorrect
1. *Substantially below*	**Stated** that: ☐ There is a negative cash balance.
2. *Below*	**Identified** that: ☐ There will be insufficient cash to relocate operations. ☐ Purchasing new equipment will require cash/financing ☐ Other
3. *Meets*	**Identified AND discussed:** ☐ Purchasing new equipment for the Ontario location will further strain cash flows ☐ The cash flow statement indicates insufficient funds for relocations. ☐ It appears the equipment for the Ontario location was purchased with current funds. ☐ Other
4. *Exceeds*	**Identified AND discussed** the available data and information **AND made a recommendation** supported by analysis, including the following: ☐ Since equipment can be leased, this may be the viable option at present to reduce risk of further cash shortages. ☐ It may be not possible to relocate operations at present due to insufficient cash flow. ☐ Financing should be sought to cover short-term cash needs. ☐ Financing must be matched to cash needs — short-term for operations and long-term for equipment purchases to avoid cash shortages. ☐ Other

impact

conclusion

practical solution

ST versus LT

In my view, "asking AJXFSI for a long-term loan" is an "Other" valid point.

financing solutions

*One must have perused the financial statements in order to identify
this issue with respect to the insufficiency of cash flows.
One must also relate the items of information to each other.*

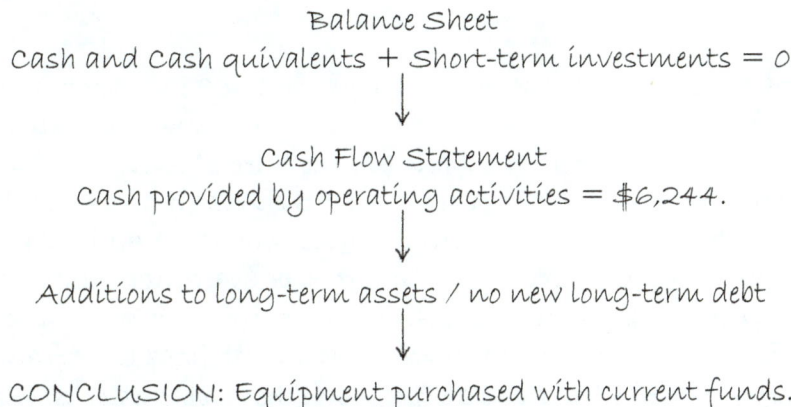

Balance Sheet
Cash and Cash quivalents + Short-term investments = 0

↓

Cash Flow Statement
Cash provided by operating activities = $6,244.

↓

Additions to long-term assets / no new long-term debt

↓

CONCLUSION: Equipment purchased with current funds.

Exhibit A – Ajax Metals

Required: "Making recommendations on the risks associated with relocating the manufacturing of the products".

− non-directed issue −

Competency Grids (continued)

A13

Core and core-related competencies   MA: Management accounting

PK:MA:03 — Identifies, assesses, and advises on information required for management decision making (cost-volume-profit relationships, cost classifications and flows, market or industry data, non-financial factors)

Baseline question: Did the candidate compare the profitability of each of the products associated with each of the segments and provide recommendations for future production?

A short calculation is presented between parentheses to better justify the ideas put forward.

Since the information is supplied per division, it is not surprising to note that the aspect of comparability is significant in the analysis.

Performance level	Solution Key
0. *NR/Inc*	Did not attempt or insufficient response to evaluate, OR incorrect
1. *Substantially below*	**Identified** that: ☐ The products vary in their profitability.
2. *Below* *calculation only*	**Discussed:** ☐ The profitability of Industrial is 40 percent (23,040 / 57,600) ☐ The profitability of Standard is 31 percent (7,496 / 24,200) ☐ The profitability of Liquified is 6 percent (1,140 / 17,840) ☐ Other
3. *Meets* *COMPARING the products to each other is necessary at the "Meets" level.*	**Discussed AND compared:** ☐ That Standard product is more profitable than Liquified and less profitable than Industrial, and it may be feasible to continue production ☐ The impact of the environment associated with each location, which can affect profitability ☐ Other
4. *Exceeds* *3 products* ↓ *3 recommendations*	**Discussed AND compared** the available data and information **AND made a recommendation** supported by the analysis, including the following: ☐ That Liquified product is the least profitable and it is not recommended to relocate this product to Ontario ☐ That Industrial product is the most profitable and it appears relocating it to Mexico may be feasible; however, the health concerns must be seriously considered first ☐ That Standard product is more profitable than Liquified and less profitable than Industrial, and it may be feasible to continue production ☐ Other

different location
↓
different environment

Note the frequent use of the terms "more profitable" and "less profitable". Note also that the "feasibility" of the planned relocations is regularly challenged.

Prior to relocating a division, it is indeed relevant to take into account the profitability of the project
+
to make sure that "public health" has been adequately considered.

Recommending that one examine in greater detail why the gross margin of the liquified product is so low would, in my opinion, be an "Other" valid point.

One could also compute the gross margin for 2009 in order to be able to compare the variation between the two years. This would, in my view, be an "Other" valid point at the "Meets" level.

However, at a glance, one observes that the gross margin is stable for the Industrial and Liquified products, whereas it diminishes for the Standard product. It would, therefore, be marginally less useful to compute the ratios for 2009. Under these circumstances, since the resolution of a case must take place within a restricted time frame, one should instead focus one's energy on other problems or issues.

Competency Grids (continued)

exhibits
1-
↓
conclusions
relocations

proposed
changes
2-
↓
cash flows

exhibits
3-
↓
conclusions
cash flows /
internal
controls

Professional qualities and skills *a*   IA: Integrative Approach

PR:IA:03 — Evaluates implications and assesses the appropriateness of solutions beyond the immediate or short term (considers potential impact of decisions on other systems and processes, such as internal controls, impact on other departments, or other functional areas)

see beyond the immediate problem ✓

Baseline question: Did the candidate ✓ integrate information from the various exhibits in order to draw conclusions regarding the changes to manufacturing locations; ✓ inform the board of the potential impacts of the proposed changes on current and future cash flows; ✓ draw conclusions from the exhibits regarding cash flows and/or internal controls?   *Integration is an essential professional quality which must be clearly demonstrated at the "Meets" level.*

Performance level	Solution Key
0. *NR/Inc*	Failed to address the competency
3. *Meets* *IMPACT*	☐ 1 **Integrated** information from the various exhibits in order to draw conclusions regarding the changes to manufacturing locations ☐ 2 **Informed** the board of the potential impacts of the proposed changes on current and future cash flows ☐ 3 **Drew conclusions** from the exhibits regarding cash flows and/or internal controls ☐ Other

INTEGRATION:
- Knowing how to use the information supplied in the Exhibits in order to assess a current issue (1-) or to justify the presence of a problem (3-).
- See the interrelationships between different issues (2-).

The two aspects appear to me to be essential at the "Meets" level.

Professional qualities and skills *b*   OE: Organizational effectiveness

LD:OE:01 — Analyzes and evaluates results and information from business activities and processes against objectives and benchmarks and advises on further action (conducts and reports on gap analysis)

Baseline question: Did the candidate identify and analyze the various issues facing the client and advise on further action?   *advises on further action* → *concrete recommendations*

Performance level	Solution Key
0. *NR/Inc*	Failed to address the competency
3. *Meets* *3 steps: ID-ANAL-REC for at least 3 PROBLEMS*	✓**Identified** aspects of at least 3 major problems, ✓**analyzed** key aspects of the issues, **AND** ✓**advised** on further action regarding the problems: ☐ Intercompany transactions will be eliminated and subsidiaries will have to pay income tax as legal entities A17 ☐ More tests on product are needed to ensure product safety A19 ☐ Tax rates should be examined to determine the benefits of moving production to another country A17 ☐ Other

REC needed at this level

ORGANIZATIONAL EFFECTIVENESS:
   Knowing how to solve a problem or issue in a structured manner, using adequate information supplied, is a professional quality which one must absolutely develop through the regular simulation of cases.

a Personally, when I award the "Meets" level for a "Professional qualities and skills" competency, I make sure that the candidate has supplied a good quality analysis.

b In my view, one must have achieved the "Exceeds" level for at least three of the significant problems or issues in order to achieve the "Meets" level.
   This is because the part "AND made a recommendation supported by the analysis" is usually required at the "Exceeds" level in the assessment of the core and core-related competencies.

Exhibit A – Ajax Metals

Competency Grids (continued)

Professional qualities and skills   *PS: Problem Solving*

PR:PS:03 — Integrates and analyzes data for patterns, relationships, and trends

Baseline question: Did the candidate form conclusions and provide recommendations regarding the profitability of products; calculate gross margins for each product and compare to others?

3 divisions
↓
3 calculations

Performance level	Solution Key
0. *NR/Inc*	Failed to address the competency
3. *Meets* *see A24*	**Identified, analyzed, AND evaluated** the behaviour of the trends or patterns in the data provided ☐ Other

In my view, achieving the "Meets" level requires:
- a calculation of the % of gross margin of EACH of the three divisions.
- a COMMENTED comparison of the % achieved between the three divisions.

Professional qualities and skills   *PS: Professional self-evaluation*

PR:SE:01 — Acts within the scope of professional competence (does not attempt to provide expert advice in areas of specialized knowledge outside own capabilities and qualifications)

Baseline question: Did the candidate identify that the international tax issues are beyond her expertise and the appropriate tax expert should be consulted?   *YES or NO?*

key concept: complexity

Performance level	Solution Key
0. *NR/Inc*	Failed to address the competency
3. *Meets*	**Identified** the issues as follows: ☐ The international tax issues, including the transfer pricing issue and new tax compliance requirements as a result of the proposed corporate structure, are complex enough that an outside tax expert should be approached for advice. ☐ Other

In my view, achieving the "Meets" level requires:
- a clear reference to the fact that the required competencies are outside the scope of professional competence.
- a clear reference to the relevant tax aspect, in light of the particulars of the case.

INTERNAL and/or EXTERNAL Stakeholders point of view

Professional qualities and skills   *SF: Stakeholder Focus*

PR:SF:01 — Anticipates and meets the needs and expectations of internal and external stakeholders

Baseline question: Did the candidate identify and analyze the various issues facing the client and advise on further action?

"Meets" level: WHY there is an issue + IMPACT of the issue

Performance level	Solution Key
0. *NR/Inc*	Failed to address the competency
3. *Meets*	**Explained** the issues and the impact: ☐ Not in public interest ☐ Potential loss of reputation due to lawsuit ☐ Other

see beyond the numbers

Reminder:
"Candidates have to demonstrate the professional competencies expected of a newly certified CGA." (CGA syllabus)

© CGA = COMPETENCY

Competency Grids (continued)

Part b

IFRS

Core and core-related competencies a   *A14 + A15*   *FA: Financial accounting*
PK:FA:02 — Evaluates, interprets, and advises on accounting policies and procedures in accordance with professional standards (standards for not-for-profit, public and private corporations, and the public sector)

Baseline question: Did the candidate explain that AJX must adopt IFRS for January 2011 and explain some of the changes necessary to restate Metallo's financial statements in accordance with IFRS?

There is more to say with respect to the differences as opposed to the similarities.

Focus: changes to comply with IFRS

Performance level	Solution Key
0. *NR/Inc*	Did not attempt or insufficient response to evaluate, OR incorrect
1. *Substantially below*	**Identified** that: ☐ Public companies must use IFRS in 2011. ☐ Some of the current accounting policies and procedures may need to be changed. ☐ There are similarities and differences between existing Canadian GAAP and IFRS.
2. *Below*	**Discussed**: ☐ Since Metallo is owned by a public company consolidation, it would be easier if its financial statements were prepared in accordance with IFRS. ☐ Since Metallo's shares are not publicly traded, the financial statements do not have to be prepared in accordance with IFRS. ☐ Other
3. *Meets* *BREADTH over DEPTH* *The comparisons between ASPE and IFRS are clearly stated.*	**Discussed AND explained**: ☑ Since the year end is November 30, 2010, IFRS must be adopted for the fiscal year beginning December 1, 2011. ☑ Mandatory adoption of IFRS is required for publicly traded entities for fiscal periods beginning on or after January 1, 2011. ☑ Earlier adoption of IFRS is permitted prior to January 1, 2011. ☐ IAS 29 requires restatement of financial statements due to hyperinflation should that occur in Mexico, which differs from current Canadian GAAP, which does not adjust for inflation. ☐ IFRS 8 requires disclosure of segment liabilities, which is not currently required in section 1701. ☐ Some specific sections of the CICA Handbook, which are converged with IAS: section 1582 with IFRS 3, section 1602 with IAS 27. ☐ IFRS have more disclosures than GAAP; for example, the section 3840 related parties' disclosures are much less comprehensive than those required by IAS 24. ☐ Other
4. *Exceeds* *ACTIONS to implement* *↓* *WHAT TO DO*	**Discussed AND explained** the available data and information **AND made a recommendation** supported by the analysis, including the following: ☐ Adopt IFRS, IAS 21 requires non-monetary items measured at fair value be translated at the date when the fair value was determined rather than the balance sheet date. ☐ Restate Metallo's financial statements in accordance with IFRS so there are comparatives available prior to mandatory adoption for AJX. ☐ Prepare an opening IFRS statement of financial position at the date of transition to IFRS. ☐ Other

IFRS
↓
IAS 16.29
↓
Cost model OR Revaluation model
↓
It is, in my view, an "Other" valid point, especially in the context where there are European buyers interested in Metallo's financial statements.

practical aspect

"Under IAS 36, there may be impairment of the recently purchased equipment that has proven to be problematic for changing package sizes."
This can be an "Other" valid point.

A connection made with the requirements of the European buyers will likely be considered at the "Exceeds" level.

---

a One must understand that professional examination cases usually take place in the current year. Consequently, the first three points at the "Meets" level (✓) would not require discussion in a case to be resolved in 2013. However, it is relevant to explain the changes which must be made to the financial statements where an entity decides to adopt IFRS.

Exhibit A – Ajax Metals

Competency Grids (continued)

Core and core-related competencies   *AS: Assurance*

PK:AS:02 — Determines and advises on whether to accept an engagement consistent with professional standards (e.g., evaluates potential clients, communicates with predecessor auditor, checks for conflict of interest)

Baseline question: Did the candidate identify and analyze specific areas that should be reviewed before the engagement is accepted?

Performance level	Solution Key
0. *NR/Inc*	Did not attempt or insufficient response to evaluate, OR incorrect
1. *Substantially below*	**Stated** that the engagement can be accepted, but did not raise any concerns
2. *Below*	**Identified** that some review of client information is required before the engagement is accepted ☐ Other
3. *Meets*	**Identified AND analyzed** specific areas that should be reviewed before the engagement is accepted, including: ☐ The lack of information for the Mexico division ☐ Potential buyer might perceive John's lack of independence ☐ Cash flow problems can lead to going concern issues. ☐ Other
4. *Exceeds*	**Identified AND analyzed** specific areas to be reviewed before the audit is accepted **AND recommended** that further investigation is required: ☐ Recommends appropriate controls to be implemented in the divisions to avoid future occurrences of the lack of information MT ☐ Recommends another auditor within the firm ☐ Recommends adequate disclosure of any material uncertainty regarding the ability of Metallo to realize its assets and discharge its liabilities ST ☐ Other

Since the financial accounting system has failed (A9), one could ask questions about the reliability of the internal control.

In my view, the ethical issue in moving manufacturing to Mexico is an item to be considered in the acceptance of the audit engagement. This is an "Other" valid point.

When there are cash flow problems, you should consider the going concern issue.

lack of information

↓

REC: appropriate controls to implement

John's lack of independence

↓

REC: another auditor within the firm

European buyers have specifically required that Metallo's financial statements be audited by a firm other than AJX's auditor. Consequently, recommending that one ask the opinion of the European buyers would not be a good solution, since there is a perceived conflict of interest that can not be avoided by John on a short-term basis.

Required: "explaining the requirements to upcoming audit"

Competency Grids (continued)

Core and core-related competencies *A15*   AS: Assurance

PK:AS:03 — Determines the scope of the engagement or management audit (contents of engagement letter, client expectation, limitations on scope, timing, signoffs)

Baseline question: Did the candidate identify that the lack of information for the Mexican division is a scope limitation and explain how this problem could be resolved?

lack of information + backups not located ↓ scope limitation

Performance level	Solution Key
0. *NR/Inc*	Did not attempt or insufficient response to evaluate, OR incorrect
1. *Substantially below*	**Stated** that ☐ There is a potential or actual scope restriction.
2. *Below* *WHY*	**Analyzed** ☐ Inability to obtain the Mexican division's records can cause a scope limitation. ☐ There are materiality aspects of the scope limitation ☐ Other
3. *Meets* *impact*	**Analyzed AND identified** that: ☐ If the missing transactions in the Mexican division are immaterial to Metallo's financial statements, an unqualified report can be issued. ☐ If the missing transactions in the Mexican division are material or pervasive, a qualified or no opinion would be issued. ☐ It is important to retrieve the Mexican division's records to avoid a scope limitation. ☐ Other
4. *Exceeds* *solutions*	**Analyzed AND identified** the available data and information **AND made a recommendation** supported by the analysis, including the following: ☐ If a backup of the transactions cannot be restored, the data must be reentered to avoid a scope limitation. *ST* ☐ Ensure appropriate controls are in place to avoid loss of data in the future, which can result in a scope limitation. *LT* ☐ Other

ISSUE "scope limitation" ↓

ANALYSIS "analyzed and identified" ↓

RECOMMEND

SO? materiality concept

see beyond the immediate problem ✓

Focus: Metallo, not AJX

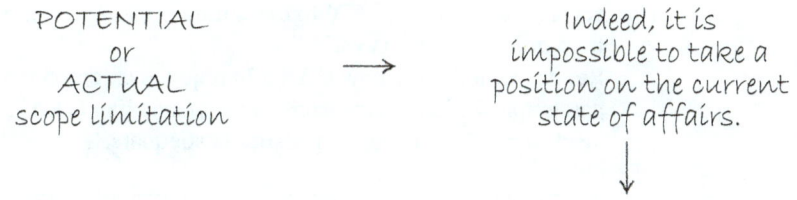

POTENTIAL
or
ACTUAL
scope limitation   →   Indeed, it is impossible to take a position on the current state of affairs.
↓

One must assess:
- if it would be possible to recover data with the backups.
- the significance of the data for the Mexico division.

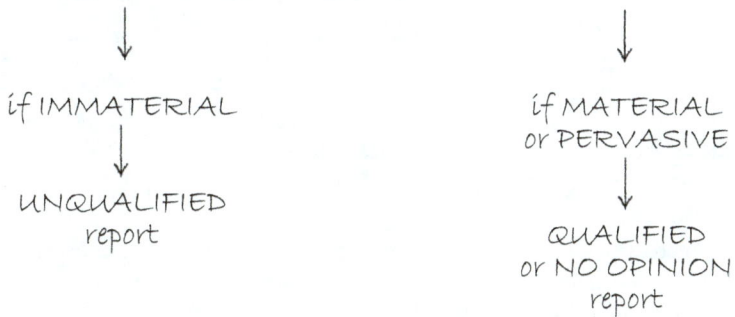

↓   ↓

if IMMATERIAL   if MATERIAL or PERVASIVE
↓   ↓

UNQUALIFIED   QUALIFIED
report   or NO OPINION
                                 report

Exhibit A – Ajax Metals

Required:
"explaining the requirements
to upcoming audit"

Competency Grids (continued)

Core and core-related competencies a   *A15*

AS: Assurance

PK:AS:04 — Evaluates risks and business issues (nature of organization, control environment) to determine their impact on the engagement or management audit (extent, materiality, nature, and timing of engagement)

Baseline question: Did the candidate explain that Metallo's current financial position may indicate a going concern problem that will require the audit report to be modified under the new Canadian Auditing Standards?

POTENTIAL
going
concern
problem
↓
need audit
evidence
↓
may impact
the
audit report
↓
GAAS
↓
going
concern
issue
adequately
disclosed
↓
unqualified
audit report

Performance level	Solution Key
0. *NR/Inc*	Did not attempt or insufficient response to evaluate, OR incorrect
1. *Substantially below*	**Identified** that: ☐ There is a potential going concern problem.
2. *Below*	**Analyzed** that: ☐ A going concern problem may impact the audit report. ☐ There is a difference between current Canadian GAAS and CAS for reporting on going concern issues. ☐ Other
3. *Meets* *GAAS versus CAS*	**Analyzed AND explained**: ☐ If Metallo reports using current Canadian GAAP, the going concern issue must be adequately disclosed and the auditor's report will be unqualified. ☐ Since the reporting period ends November 30, 2010, Metallo will not be subject to examination under the new CAS, which is implemented for audits of financial statements for periods ending on or after December 14, 2010. ☐ There are indicators of a going concern problem, which must be considered in conducting the audit and issuing the report. ☐ Other
4. *Exceeds* *consequences*	**Analyzed AND explained** the available data and information **AND made a recommendation** supported by the analysis, including the following: ☐ Risk-assessment procedures must be conducted per CAS 315 in accordance with CAS 570 to determine if management's assumption for a going concern is valid. ☐ Reporting under the new CAS 570 requires an emphasis of matter paragraph, which differs from current Canadian GAAS, even when disclosure of going concern issues is adequate. *CAS 570.18-20* ☐ Other

We do not know, for the time being, if the Going concern assumption is appropriate or not. Since the cash flow problem can be explained by the mismatching of financing with investment, it may be that this a temporary situation. However, the auditor must obtain evidence in the conduct of the audit on the entity's ability to continue as a going concern.

If use of the going concern assumption is appropriate + material uncertainty exists

↓   ↓

if adequate disclosure made   *If adequate disclosure is NOT made*

↓   ↓

UNMODIFIED opinion
+
Emphasis of Matter paragraph
in the auditor's report

QUALIFIED OPINION
OR
ADVERSE OPINION

"Other" valid point?
a procedure...
- "See evidence that Metallo has found long term financing for the equipment."
- "Enquire with Metallo as to their plan to find new customers/ new markets in places where sales are expected to decrease significantly."
- Etc.

---

a *A going concern problem is a risky issue which is sometimes difficult to assess for an auditor. Personally, I believe that it would be preferable to follow the CAS rather the GAAS. Since the auditor is responsible for ensuring a fair presentation of the financial statements, it appears to me to be wise to follow the more stringent standards.*

Competency Grids (continued)

Required:
"explaining the requirements
to upcoming audit"

Core and core-related competencies　A15　　ET: Ethics and trust

PR:ET:03 — Maintains objectivity and independence in appearance and fact (avoids real and perceived conflicts of interest)

concept:
perceived
conflict of
interest

Baseline question: Did the candidate explain there is a perceived conflict of interest for John to act as audit manager in the audit of Metallo?

Performance level	Solution Key
0. *NR/Inc*	Did not attempt or insufficient response to evaluate, OR incorrect
1. *Substantially below*	**Restated** the facts of the case related to the issues of objectivity and independence, without elaboration: ☐ There is a conflict of interest. ☐ CGAs are bound to follow CEPROC.
2. *Below* *clear* *conclusions*	**Identified** the issues: ☐ There is a conflict of interest for John to work on the audit of Metallo. ☐ Megan is not acting ethically by engaging John to audit Metallo. ☐ Other
3. *Meets* *consequences*	**Identified** the issues AND **explained** the impact: ☐ The European buyers may perceive a conflict of interest for John to act as audit manager in the audit of Metallo. ☐ John may not be truly objective in auditing Metallo because in working on the audit of AJX, he may have previously examined Metallo's records. ☐ John's conflict of interest may be perceived or actual. ☐ Other
4. *Exceeds* *clear* *recommendations*	**Identified** the issues, **explained** the impact, **AND made a recommendation** supported by the analysis, including the following: ☐ John's conflict of interest and recommends he remove himself from the audit. ☐ Recommended appointing another audit manager within ALN Canada ☐ Other

public
accountant
↓
objectivity
+
independence

European
buyers have
specifically
required
Metallo's
financial
statements
audited by
a firm other
than AJX's
auditor.

ethical
issue
↓
CEPROC

WHY

safeguards

It is true that John lacks the necessary independence to perform the tasks requested by Megan. However, in the context of a case, John must nevertheless respond to all the questions required under b.

One should note that the ethical question is raised regarding the two CGA protagonists in the case, namely Megan and John.
On the one hand, Megan should not have considered hiring John in order to audit Metallo and,
on the other hand, John cannot accept this offer.
THE PERSON MAKING THE OFFER and THE PERSON RECEIVING THE OFFER are both responsible for their conduct.

The ethics and trust issues are important in our profession.
Noting the existence of a problem only allows you to achieve the "Below" level.
What is important is knowing why,
in light of the particulars of the case, the problem exists.
As a future CGA professional, you must be aware of this, which explains the requirements at the "Meets" level.
Finally, one must submit clear recommendations with a view to eliminating, or mitigating, any problem raised.
N.B.: This comment also applies to the ethical issue appearing on A20.

Come decision time, one is usually required to use the information supplied in the case in order to analyze the situation, in light of its benefits and disadvantages. In the context of the adoption of the IFRS, the identification of the similarities and differences between the two financial reporting frameworks will enable AJX to make an informed decision.

Competency Grids (continued)

Professional qualities and skills   IA: Integrative Approach

PR:IA:01 — Aggregates information from a variety of sources and perspectives to assess the impact of issues on the organization

Baseline question: Did the candidate identify the similarities and differences between current Canadian GAAP and IFRS and inform the board of directors of some of the requirements in meeting the new standards? Did the candidate inform or provide recommendations regarding the adoption of IFRS by Metallo?   *YES or NO?*

similarities + differences

Performance level	Solution Key
0. *NR/Inc*	Failed to address the competency
3. *Meets* *see A27*	**Identified** similarities and differences between Canadian GAAP and IFRS, **analyzed, AND evaluated** the similarities and differences, **AND identified** issues involved in the decision to adopt IFRS. ☐ Other

N.B.: The two following professional qualities Communication are usually overall competencies which assess both Parts a. and b. of the case.

Personally, I give the level "Meets" to the candidate who communicates his response without making "major mistakes."

Professional qualities and skills   CM: Communication

same audience
↓
2 letters
↓
2 different signatures

PR:CM:02 Prepares information in formats appropriate for specific purposes (audit reports, memos, management letters, consulting reports, financial reports)

Baseline question: Did the candidate write a letter using appropriate characteristics?

Performance level	Solution Key
0. *NR/Inc*	Failed to address the competency
3. *Meets* *2/3 characteristics*	In the requested format and had 2 key characteristics. Key characteristics: *LANGUAGE: Simple, precise and unambiguous wording, complete ideas, reasonable abbreviations, professional language, etc.* ☐ Appropriate tone ☐ Appropriate language ☐ Well-organized ☐ Other

TONE: Since the memo is addressed to the board of directors, there is no need to explain current business terms such as "backup."

ORGANIZATION: Appropriate presentation, titles and subtitles, structured discussion, conclusions or recommendations that stand out clearly, appropriate references, etc.

Professional qualities and skills   CM: Communication

one idea
↓
one complete sentence

PR:CM:03 — Communicates information in a timely, clear, and concise manner (explains quantitative and qualitative information in language adapted to various stakeholders)

Baseline question: Did the candidate communicate the issues identified in the case to the appropriate people in a timely, clear, and concise manner?

THE RESOLUTION OF PROBLEMS OR ISSUES NEEDS TO BE STRUCTURED LOGICALLY.

Performance level	Solution Key
0. *NR/Inc*	Failed to address the competency
3. *Meets*	Answer was understandable (logical) AND written in a clear and concise manner, such that the assessor needed to make *few* assumptions.

"Clear" and "concise" are the key words!

Logical/Coherent ideas.

The text of the response must flow well.

The assessor needs to understand what he is reading without having to wonder "what did the candidate mean?" He cannot make presumptions about something that is not there in writing. The assessor who reads your response without having to wonder about the understandability of the ideas contained therein will probably award the "Meets" level.

© CGA = COMPETENCY